BETTER THAN CARROTS OR STICKS

ASCD MEMBER BOOK

Many ASCD members received this book as a
member benefit upon its initial release.

Learn more at: **www.ascd.org/memberbooks**

DOMINIQUE
SMITH

DOUGLAS
FISHER

NANCY
FREY

BETTER THAN CARROTS OR STICKS

Restorative Practices for Positive Classroom Management

ASCD | Alexandria, VA USA

1703 N. Beauregard St. • Alexandria, VA 22311-1714 USA
Phone: 800-933-2723 or 703-578-9600 • Fax: 703-575-5400
Website: www.ascd.org • E-mail: member@ascd.org
Author guidelines: www.ascd.org/write

Judy Seltz, *Executive Director;* Stefani Roth, *Publisher;* Genny Ostertag, *Director, Content Acquisitions;* Julie Houtz, *Director, Book Editing & Production;* Ernesto Yermoli, *Editor;* Lindsey Smith, *Senior Graphic Designer;* Mike Kalyan, *Manager, Production Services;* Cindy Stock, *Production Designer;* Kelly Marshall, *Production Specialist*

PAPERBACK ISBN: 978-1-4166-2062-4   ASCD product #116005
Quantity discounts: 10–49, 10%; 50+, 15%; 1,000+, special discounts (e-mail programteam@ascd.org or call 800-933-2723, ext. 5773, or 703-575-5773). Also available in e-book formats. For desk copies, go to www.ascd.org/deskcopy.

ASCD Member Book No. FY15-12A (Aug. 2015 P). Member books mail to Premium (P), Select (S), and Institutional Plus (I+) members on this schedule: Jan, PSI+; Feb, P; Apr, PSI+; May, P; Jul, PSI+; Aug, P; Sep, PSI+; Nov, PSI+; Dec, P. For details, see www.ascd.org/membership and www.ascd.org/memberbooks.

Library of Congress Cataloging-in-Publication Data

Smith, Dominique.
    Better than carrots or sticks : restorative practices for positive classroom management / Dominique Smith, Douglas Fisher, Nancy Frey.
        pages cm
    Includes bibliographical references and index.
    ISBN 978-1-4166-2062-4 (pbk. : alk. paper) 1. Classroom management. 2. Peace—Study and teaching. 3. School discipline. 4. Restorative justice. I. Fisher, Douglas, 1965– II. Frey, Nancy, 1959– III. Title.
    LB3013.S596 2015
    371.102′4—dc23
                                                    2015017563

23 22 21 20 19 18 17 16   4 5 6 7 8 9 10 11 12

Contents

1 | Punitive or Restorative: The Choice Is Yours

A colleague of ours once projected the following quote, widely attributed to Frederick Douglass, onto a screen at the start of a professional development session: *start well*

(It is easier to build strong children than to repair broken men.)

She then asked the assembled faculty to write down their own reactions to the statement and discuss them in small groups. The reactions our colleague heard were both positive and predictable: a lot of talk about the influence of students' family, school climate, and a sense of connectedness within the school on academic achievement.

When the conversations drew to a close, our colleague shared the school's discipline data from the previous year, which showed that suspensions occurred at rates disproportionate to the student population. In a majority of cases, the most serious offense was identified as *defiance*—a nonviolent act, and one that is broad and vaguely defined. This is not an uncommon finding: According to a report of suspensions in California schools, 34 percent of suspended students were punished for defiance or disruption (Losen, Martinez, & Okelola, 2014). Our administrator friend had calculated the number of instructional days lost to suspensions and provided comparative data on

vague & nebulous

1

the grade point averages of suspended students versus those who had never been suspended. She then asked the faculty whether they were building strong children or ensuring that their communities will have future broken adults in need of repair. The frank 30-minute discussion that ensued inspired the school's staff to create a culture in which restorative practices could thrive. Over countless department meetings and informal exchanges, the staff performed yeomen's work analyzing and redefining classroom and schoolwide practices.

Our own experience has been that while our collective hearts as educators are in the right place, we tend to make decisions based on past experience. After all, we began our on-the-job training as teachers when we were five years old. Our beliefs about school, classroom management, and discipline have been shaped by decades of experience, starting in kindergarten. What we need is an effective classroom-management system—one that we can hold onto in times of stress and strife.

Effective Classroom Management

The term *classroom management* is confusing and misleading, mainly because it has no clear and widely agreed-upon definition. For some, the term refers to general control of students; for others, it refers to discipline procedures; for others still, it refers to both routines and procedures. Up until recently, we have avoided using the term, but we finally came across a definition we could stand behind: Cassetta and Sawyer (2013) define classroom management as being "about building relationships with students and teaching social skills along with academic skills" (p. 16), and we couldn't agree more.

There are two aspects of an effective learning environment (and, by extension, successful classroom management): *relationships* (specifically, the range of interpersonal skills necessary to maintain healthy relationships) and *high-quality instruction*. When students have strong, trusting relationships both with the adults in the school and

C.M = relationships + teaching social & academic

with their peers, and when their lessons are interesting and relevant, ~~it's harder for them to misbehave~~. *relationships & engagement*

We don't expect an effective classroom-management system to eliminate all problematic behavior any more than we expect a new set of standards to raise all students' scores by leaps and bounds on the first try. Students are going to misbehave as they learn and grow—it's how we respond to their misbehavior that matters. We believe that students should have a chance to learn from their mistakes and to restore any damaged relationships with others. Our view is known as the restorative approach to discipline. The table in Figure 1.1, developed by the San Francisco Unified School District, illustrates

trad. vs. restorative approaches have different values

1.1 Traditional Versus Restorative Approach to Discipline

Traditional Approach	Restorative Approach
• Schools and rules are violated. • Justice focuses on establishing guilt. • Accountability is defined as punishment. • Justice is directed at the offender; the victim is ignored. • Rules and intent outweigh the outcome. • No opportunity is offered for the offender to express remorse or make amends.	• People and relationships are violated. • Justice identifies needs and obligations. • Accountability is defined as understanding the effects of the offense and repairing any harm. • The offender, victim, and school all have direct roles in the justice process. • Offenders are held responsible for their behavior, repairing any harm they've caused and working toward a positive outcome. • Opportunities are offered for offenders to express remorse or make amends.

Source: Adapted from San Francisco Unified School District. (n.d.). Restorative practices whole-school implementation guide (p. 19). San Francisco, CA: Author.

the differences between the restorative approach and the traditional approach to discipline.

The Restorative Practices Movement in Schools

[handwritten margin note: connection to restorative justice]

In its contemporary incarnation, the restorative practices movement is an offshoot of the restorative justice model used by courts and law-enforcement agencies around the world. In the restorative justice model, mutually consenting victims and offenders meet so that the former can be given a voice and the latter can have an opportunity to make amends. Importantly, this approach empowers a community to take an active role in resolving problems. Cultures throughout the world employ restorative justice to create peace among adversaries, ensure restitution, and make decisions at times of community crisis.

Restorative practices in schools cast a wider net than restorative justice in the courts. Whereas justice is by its nature reactive, restorative practices also include preventive measures designed to build skills and capacity in students as well as adults.

[handwritten margin note: I mean I don't think that distributive justice would restore empowerment NEED justice]

Restorative practices are predicated on the positive relationships that students and adults have with one another. Simply said, it's harder for students to act defiantly or disrespectfully toward adults who clearly care about them and their future. Healthy and productive relationships between and among students and staff facilitate a positive school climate and learning environment. In the restorative approach, when relationships in the school become damaged, the parties involved are encouraged to engage in reflective conversations that help offenders understand the harm that their actions caused and provide them with opportunities to make amends. As we describe further in this book, there are a number of ways to build relationships and create healthy learning communities.

Circles. Teachers in the restorative practices movement promote a sense of family in the classroom by having students sit in circles to discuss both curriculum-related topics (e.g., the role of genocide and war in a World History class) and noncurricular issues that bear discussing (e.g., how students might manage stress on the eve of a major state exam).

Individual conferences to address problematic behavior. We'll explore the details of these high-stakes meetings in greater detail further in the book, but for now know that restorative practices are not about letting things go or ignoring when harm has been done. Individual conferences require intense preparation on the part of the victim(s), the perpetrator(s), witnesses to the conflict, and anyone else who's been affected by it. In some cases, conferences involve two sets of parents or guardians who are very much at odds with each other: it's common for the offender's family to lobby for mercy and for the victim's family to demand retribution. To ensure that conferences run smoothly, it is crucial to engage with families preventively, before crises occur.

[handwritten margin note: do not ignore problems]

The criminal justice system. In a small number of cases, the criminal justice system will play an important part in a restorative approach to student discipline. We have found that strong ties to our local police department and juvenile justice system have enhanced our ability to play a meaningful role in the lives of adjudicated youth, allowing us to partner with families and the courts to positively affect students' lives. In fact, many youth court systems follow the restorative approach to justice, which mandates therapeutic interventions over retributive ones. We have personally been fortunate to work with skilled police and youth probation officers who have received formal training in restorative practices.

Teaching Rather than Punishing

Traditional school discipline practices are considered separate from the academic mission of the school. By contrast, *restorative practices are interwoven into every interaction in the building*. At your

[handwritten note: integrated approaches]

school, is a specific administrator assigned to disciplinary matters? This might be the principal, vice principal, or dean of students. Ask a few students at your school, "Where do kids go when they misbehave?" If you keep hearing a specific person's name—or worse, a specific *practice* (e.g., "Kids go home 'cause they get suspended")—then you know that your school is pursuing a traditional approach to discipline. If this is the case, it's time for a change.

It's far too common in schools for educators to wait for discipline problems to emerge and then handle them on a case-by-case basis. Such an approach leaves adults exhausted and children with limited skills development. We don't leave the acquisition of reading or mathematics skills to chance; we engage in explicit, systematic, and intentional instruction to ensure that learners progress academically. So why wouldn't we do the same to ensure that students progress socially and emotionally? The social and emotional development of students is often poorly articulated in schools—relegated to an assembly and a few accompanying lessons. Traditional tools for addressing behavioral issues among students—rewards and consequences, shame and humiliation, suspensions and expulsions—run counter to a restorative culture and do not result in lasting change, much less a productive learning environment.

Rewards and Consequences Don't Work

Right now you may be thinking to yourself: *I've got a whole list of rewards and consequences in place to manage behavior.* To be sure, nearly every classroom-management book will have a section devoted to the use of rewards and consequences. But there's one problem: *Rewards and consequences don't work*—or at least, they don't *teach.* They may result in short-term changes, but in reality they promote compliance and little else.

[handwritten margin note: a commitment to teaching humans]

[handwritten note: rewards don't teach]

Rewards

You may be thinking to yourself: *I don't use punishments. My students earn points and privileges for good behavior.* Some people think that bribing students with an ice-cream social or a movie day when they behave is somehow better than meting out consequences when they don't. In reality, rewards and consequences are two sides of the same coin: both are attempts to control students' behavior rather than teach them how to engage in productive learning. Tangible rewards have actually been shown to undermine motivation (Deci, Koestner, & Ryan, 2001). Rewards suggest to people that they are being compensated for engaging in an unpleasant obligation. Importantly, research shows that good behavior diminishes as rewards are phased out. According to Kohn (2010), "Scores of studies have confirmed that rewards tend to lead people to lose interest in whatever they had to do to snag them. This principle has been replicated with many different populations (across genders, ages, and nationalities) and with a variety of tasks as well as different kinds of inducements (money, As, food, and praise, to name four)" (p. 17). Because students begin to lose interest with what they're doing, over time the number or value of the rewards offered to them must increase if they are to remain on task.

[handwritten margin note: rewards "/ teaching becomes ineffective (ahem... PAW perks...)]

Consequences

Why do we punish students by meting out "consequences" when they misbehave? Probably because we experienced punishment as students ourselves. The most common punishment for student misbehavior in elementary school is loss of recess (Moberly, Waddle, & Duff, 2005)—ironic, given that evidence has shown regular physical activity to reduce problematic behavior and increase student achievement (Ratey, 2008). Another common punishment: placing students' names on a board and applying checkmarks by those of students who've misbehaved. Such attempts to hold students publicly accountable for their behavior can render them compliant but can also make them feel anger, humiliation, and a range of other negative emotions that serve to shut down learning (Woolfolk Hoy & Weinstein, 2006).

Taking things away from students in the name of improving their behavior and learning can actually do the exact opposite. Can you imagine if we did the same in an attempt to improve faculty behavior? What if you had to stay 10 minutes after work because you talked during a staff meeting? What if your name were singled out on a chart for turning your grades in late? Consider the range of emotions these actions would evoke in you—and realize that children feel these emotions, too.

empathy for our students

Nancy remembers her first year teaching elementary school. She had taken a classroom-management course as part of her teacher-preparation program, written papers about her philosophy of teaching, and investigated various different management systems. In her student-teaching class, for example, she observed a "stoplight" classroom-management system in which students' names were written on slips of paper and placed in color-coded card stock pock-

ets: green for good behavior, yellow for behavior that had led to a warning, and red for misbehavior that needed to be addressed. When Nancy was hired for her first teaching position, she adopted a similar practice: labeling clothespins with students' names and moving them along a cardboard continuum that ranged from "Outstanding" to "Office." However, it soon became apparent to Nancy that moving clothespins all day long consumed a lot of time that she could otherwise devote to teaching. What's more, the clothespin system had led to little change in her students' behavior; in fact, the children lost interest in the system—and, soon after, in learning. Instead of fewer challenging behaviors, Nancy seemed to be dealing with more.

Maybe it's just not the right system, she thought. As a new teacher, she was granted release time to observe teachers at work in other classrooms, so she decided to visit the room of a veteran kindergarten teacher known around the school for her kindness and gentle nature. On observation, however, Nancy found that the teacher's classroom-management system belied her reputation. At the beginning of the school year, she had invited her students to bring their favorite stuffed animals with them to keep in class. The stuffed animals were displayed on a shelf, each one labeled with the name of its owner. Whenever students misbehaved, they were to walk to the shelf and turn their stuffed animals around to face the wall. The looks on students' faces after doing this displayed heartbreaking sadness and anger.

Nancy removed the clothespins from her classroom the very next day. She also got rid of the time-out chair. It had dawned on her that the "consequences" she was meting out were actually *punishments*— and punishments don't teach, they just create more distance between teachers and students. Punishments rely on our ability as adults to leverage an unequal power relationship over children; it puts children in their places by reminding them who's *really* in charge. Students who are punished will come up with a list of reasons why *they* are the victims and will channel their negative emotion toward those doing the punishing. Instead of reflecting on their behavior or making amends, they will plot how to avoid detection the next time. As Toner (1986) notes, punishment thwarts the development of empathy in children, who learn instead to look out for themselves regardless of their effects on others. Most troubling of all, punished children learn from adult examples that exerting power is the way for them to get what they want—a notion diametrically opposed to the social and emotional well-being we are trying to foster.

we are conditioning the wrong behavior

A Different Way Forward

It took several years, but Nancy eventually developed new tools to use with students when their behavior proved problematic. She began to spend more time establishing and teaching rules and setting expectations, structuring conversations with students that strengthened relationships and helped develop communication skills, and learning new ways to de-escalate disruptive events. Most importantly, she learned (and continues to learn) that *problematic behaviors signal a student's lack of skills for responding appropriately to difficult situations.* Just as students need teachers to teach them grammar and math, they need us to teach them how to respond properly to events.

Children who are habitually criticized, humiliated, or shamed internalize negative feelings about themselves that hinder their healthy development. By contrast, children accustomed to loving support and guidance are much more likely to become healthy and productive citizens. The traditional consequences-and-rewards system of discipline common in many classrooms is not resulting in children who are prepared to learn.

Let's be clear: we're not saying that teachers should completely refrain from rewarding students—just that the rewards should not be contingent on students' behavior. These types of rewards fall under the rubric of "noncontingent reinforcement" (Cipani & Schock, 2010). It's fine to offer rewards "just because," regardless of whether students "deserve" them or not. In fact, noncontingent reinforcement can actually help to prevent problematic behaviors: Have you ever noticed the way kindergarten teachers will sometimes place the most attention-seeking children on their laps when reading aloud to the whole class? This is a classic example of noncontingent reinforcement employed to preempt any disruption. Teachers use noncontingent reinforcement regularly as they build the culture and climate of their classrooms.

misbehavior is a cue that the student lacks a skill

what does this look like?

b/c you are receiving reinforcement at fixed times regardless, you don't feel pressure to seek it.

Shame and Humiliation Don't Work

At any moment in any class, a student may become inattentive or distracted and need to be reengaged. When you have 30 people or more in the same room, order is continuously established, lost, and restored again. People who are not educators marvel at teachers' ability to turn dozens of children into a cohesive unit. When the class is really rolling, we recognize that we're teaching with a sense of urgency that our students share.

Of course, things can and will go wrong—our brief attempt at redirecting an inattentive student won't work, or students will refuse to follow our clear directions. Being human, we might find ourselves lapsing into sarcasm or speaking more harshly than necessary. For a minority of teachers, responding in this way becomes an unfortunate habit, turning them into "the mean teachers" whom students know to avoid lest they be run roughshod over. These are the teachers whose students are often lined up near the playground fence because they've been docked a few minutes of recess for misbehaving—a public humiliation reminiscent of the pillory in medieval town squares. Perhaps you count such teachers as colleagues—and perhaps you disagree with their approach to discipline but feel that it's not your place to say anything. Unfortunately, the actions of a single teacher can negatively affect an entire school's climate: not only is the use of shame and humiliation to punish students toxic, but it's also highly infectious, spreading through a grade level or department at an alarming rate.

To be clear, we don't believe that teachers who use shame and humiliation as tools are intent on crushing the spirits of their students; we simply believe that they've mistakenly bought into the conventional wisdom that exalts punishment as an effective means of altering behavior. We are not talking here about necessary corrective discipline but, rather, of punishments specifically intended to make children "feel guilty, humiliated, or fearful in an attempt to get them to change their behavior" (Hall, 2013, p. 25).

Many of us have been on the receiving end of such punishments. For example, Doug recalls the time one of his high school teachers told him, in front of the whole class, that he'd only ever be able to work at a fast-food restaurant for the rest of his life; when he reacted with anger, the teacher punished him for it. For her part, Nancy can recall being spanked by her 1st grade teacher for neglecting to put her completed worksheet in the right place on the windowsill. No doubt the teachers in these two examples thought they were doing us a favor with their punishments—teaching us lessons that would stay with us in life. Decades later, the only lesson we learned was to associate these teachers' classrooms with feelings of anger and fear.

Given the modeling with which they're presented, it's no surprise that many children learn to resolve problems themselves using rewards and consequences—through bullying, for instance. As educators, we invest a lot of attention in teaching students to refrain from hurting their classmates. But when we misuse our power trying to do this, we map a path for students to follow that is the opposite of what we intend. Cyberbullying is one such path that has become increasingly popular among students. Unwelcome as they are, the swift repercussions of digital cruelties have had at least one positive outcome: they have focused society's attention on the serious damage that bullying—behavior learned from "consequences" absorbed earlier in life—can cause, no matter what form it takes. It's becoming less common to encounter educators who associate bullying exclusively with the rites of childhood or who dismiss it as a gender-based trait ("You know how girls are," "Boys will be boys"). Exposure to the effects of bullying behavior has led to parents and students demanding that educators intervene when it occurs. For our part as educators, we need to examine our daily interactions with students and ask ourselves whether we ourselves allow a form of bullying to occur in the name of discipline.

Intense implications of "discipline" — what are our responses modeling?

Suspensions and Expulsions Don't Work

Rates of suspension and expulsion have increased dramatically since schools began implementing zero-tolerance (ZT) policies in the mid-1990s. These policies evolved from the 1994 GunsFree Schools Act, which required districts to expel any student in possession of a weapon at school. In short order, many districts expanded the policy to cover a variety of non-weapons-related violations, including possession or use of drugs and alcohol, physical altercations, damage to school property, and multiple violations within a single academic year (Hoffman, 2014). Today, the list of offenses for which some schools have ZT policies in place includes truancy, tobacco use, and a cluster of behaviors described as "defiance." One researcher has described the proliferation of ZT policies as "the criminalization of what many consider to be typical adolescent behavior" (Jones, 2013, p. 741). Although a focus on safety is certainly laudable, the unintended effects of ZT policies—soured school climates, higher dropout rates, and lower performance on measures of student achievement (Skiba & Rausch, 2006)—are not. Another troubling aspect of ZT policies is the fact that they disproportionally affect certain demographic subgroups of students. Black and Native American children, students with disabilities, and males of all backgrounds are overrepresented in national suspension and expulsion data (Hoffman, 2014; Jones, 2013; see Figure 1.2). If you are a black or Native American child with a disability, the likelihood that you will be suspended or expelled from school is astronomical—25 percent for boys and 20 percent for girls.

As the data in Figure 1.2 show, even preschool children are being suspended from schools. It's hard for us to imagine what violations three- and four-year-olds might commit that would warrant an extended removal from the learning environment. Many caring administrators have expressed frustration at board policies that require them to mete out such harsh punishments; their professional training has taught them to see the child first—to respond in ways that teach, not punish. Policies that mandate exclusionary punishments rob educators of the ability to make child- and family-centered decisions.

More than anyone, teachers understand how vital it is for students to be present in class each day. When we suspend and expel, we

1.2 Suspension and Expulsion Data Released by the U.S. Department of Education Office for Civil Rights in 2014

- Black students are three times more likely to be suspended or expelled than white students.

- Females of color (black, Native American, and Native Alaskan) are suspended at a rate of 12 percent, compared to 2 percent for white girls.

- Students with disabilities represent 12 percent of the school-age population, but comprise 58 percent of students placed in seclusion and 75 percent of those who are physically restrained.

- Black children represent 18 percent of preschool enrollment, but 48 percent of preschool children receiving more than one out-of-school suspension. By contrast, white students represent 43 percent of preschool enrollment, but only 26 percent of preschool children receiving more than one out-of-school suspension.

- Boys represent 54 percent of preschool enrollment, but 79 percent of preschool children suspended once and 82 percent of those suspended multiple times.

Source: U.S. Department of Education Office for Civil Rights. (2014). *Civil rights data collection: Data snapshot: School discipline.* Available: http://www2.ed.gov/about/offices/list/ocr/docs/crdc-discipline-snapshot.pdf

undercut our own efforts to boost attendance. Research shows that regular school attendance in the early grades is an excellent predictor of 3rd and 5th grade reading levels (Chang & Romero, 2008) and that a student's 9th grade attendance levels can predict whether or not he or she will graduate high school (Roderick, Kelley-Kemple, Johnson, & Beechum, 2014).

When we speak of chronic absences (defined as missing more than 10 percent of the school year), how often do we consider the extent to which existing discipline policies have made the problem worse? According to Skiba (2000), 95 percent of out-of-school suspensions are for nonviolent infractions such as chronic tardiness or "willful defiance." Every child and adult has a right to feel safe and secure in school, but instituting banishments for minor infractions doesn't contribute to the well-being of anyone involved, prevents learning from occurring, and compromises the school climate.

The negative effects of suspension and explusion are not limited to students who directly receive the punishment. In a large-scale study of exclusionary discipline practices, Perry and Morris (2014) found that "higher levels of exclusionary discipline within schools over time generate collateral damage, negatively affecting the academic achievement of nonsuspended students in punitive contexts" (p. 1067). In other words, when schools rely on exclusionary disciplinary policies, the achievement of all students is negatively affected.

Building a Strong School Climate Through Restorative Practices

We all understand the need for safe schools—not only physically but psychologically as well. Too often, exchanges in schools serve to tear people down—think of the girl who is shunned in the lunchroom by students she thought were friends or the boy receiving anonymous messages on social media urging him to harm himself. As adults, we shake our heads and tell each other that, unpleasant though it is, bullying is a natural developmental phase. If a child or parent challenges us to intervene, we might bring the parties involved together to try forging a conclusion, but most of the time we're left with the lingering feeling that the conflict isn't over for good.

Of course, it's always the big stuff that gets the most attention—a big fight between two groups of students, for example, or any kind of altercation that involves law enforcement. If the event becomes publicized outside of school—especially if it involves any number of factors related to gender, race, language, disability, or sexual orientation—then district or community spokespersons can be expected to announce their opinions of staff and students alike without ever setting foot on school grounds. If a school gets enough negative publicity, it risks becoming a punching bag for the district or region. Even without a media-grabbing incident, a school can earn notoriety: by having the lowest graduation rate in the district, for example, or the worst results on state tests, or high turnover rates among teachers and administrators.

I wouldn't make it anywhere else!

Maybe your school doesn't stand out in a bad way—achievement is solidly in the middle of the pack, there hasn't been a major crisis in a long time, and students and teachers go about their business without much friction. But does the school parking lot become empty mere minutes after the school day ends? Do most students choose off-campus activities over school clubs? Do staff members see each other only rarely outside of mandatory meetings? If the answer to any of these questions is yes, then you are burdened with a weak

we don't have an effective climate

school climate MATTERS

school climate. The National Center for School Climate defines climate as the "quality and character of school life." It isn't something separate from the rest of the school; rather, it emanates from the relationships that exist between and among staff, students, family, and community. It is affected by the way discipline is handled in the school—how (and whether) problems are addressed.

BIG IMPLICATIONS

School climate informs the way teachers manage their classrooms. Positive school climate is associated with a myriad of achievement, efficacy, and health measures, such as

- Higher mathematics achievement for K–3 students (Bodovski, Nahum-Shani, & Walsh, 2013),
- Higher academic optimism among teachers (Kilinç, 2013),
- Lower body mass index scores for elementary students (Gilstad-Hayden et al., 2014), and
- Lower smoking rates among high school students (Lovato et al., 2013).

We could list other studies, but you get the idea—school climate matters; it informs how we work, teach, learn, and live. Unfortunately, it can be quite difficult to assess your school's climate from the inside. In addition, school climate isn't static—it shifts from day to day, depending on a variety of factors (e.g., who's present and who's absent, what happened over the weekend, whether the school is in the midst of statewide testing, how close the school year is to ending).

Here are just a few of the compelling reasons why it is worthwhile to focus your attention and effort on improving your school's climate using the restorative approach:

- Because you care about student achievement
- Because you care about students' civil rights
- Because you care about students' emotional and psychological health

- Because you know that students can't learn adequately if they're not in school
- Because you are alarmed at the unintended messages that we send to students using a traditional approach to discipline
- Because you know we are raising a generation of people who will one day make decisions about our own well-being later in life

Regardless of motivation, it is in our collective best interests to create safe places to work, teach, and learn.

The U.S. Department of Education (2014) has identified the following guiding principles for improving school climate:

1. Create positive climates and focus on prevention;
2. Develop clear, appropriate, and consistent expectations and consequences to address disruptive student behaviors; and
3. Ensure fairness, equity, and continuous improvement. (p. 1)

A three-pronged approach is essential—if one of the three components is missing, balance is compromised.

Schoolwide Positive Behavior Interventions and Supports and Restorative Practices

Schoolwide Positive Behavior Interventions and Supports (SWPBIS) and restorative practices are sometimes mistakenly viewed as mutually exclusive initiatives. Nothing could be further from the truth. In fact, the two can complement each another quite well: Whereas the SWPBIS approach emphasizes the prevention of problematic behavior and attention to its functions, a restorative approach focuses on problem solving (Sprague & Nelson, 2012). SWPBIS provides schools with a means for evaluating student behaviors and identifying their function, eliminating the conditions that trigger unwanted behaviors, and teaching replacement behaviors. There are three tiers to the SWPBIS approach:

[handwritten margin note: BIG PRIORITIES]

- **Tier 1:** This tier refers to the use of preventative behavioral supports across classrooms that generally meet the needs of about 80 percent of students.
- **Tier 2:** This tier refers to supports designed for the approximately 15 percent of students who misbehave frequently and require extended attention.
- **Tier 3:** This tier refers to interventions designed for the small number of students with intractable behavioral difficulties that are especially taxing to the school's resources. Supports in Tier 3 include more time-intensive tools than the other two tiers, such as functional behavioral assessments.

The restorative approach to discipline incorporates principles of the SWPBIS approach to focus on prevention through relationship building by drawing on the collective strengths of the community to help individuals in trouble regain their footing in a nurturing environment with consistent classroom practices and high expectations. Most of all, restorative practices draw their strength from communication tools: adults use language that builds agency and identity and facilitate class discussions in a way that encourages affiliation and resolves problems. Restorative practices represent a positive step forward in helping all students learn to resolve disagreements, take ownership of their behavior, and engage in acts of empathy and forgiveness.

truly "tier 1" approaches

Student Voices: "Your Kids Are Lucky to Have You"

Each chapter in this book ends with a "Student Voices" section. We frankly couldn't imagine writing a book about restorative practices without including student perspectives—after all, they are our "clients," "buying" what we have to "sell," and every good business talks regularly to its customers to find out what's working and to improve what isn't.

Sephun came to us as a good student—he got great grades and was polite in class—but one who was also content to move through school without making much of an impression. Many students are like Sephun: they come to school, do what is asked of them and no more, and leave without being noticed. However, over time, Sephun came to discover that he could thrive as an agent for change. In the 9th grade, his contributions to class discussions earned him a reputation for being insightful, serious, and mature. By 10th grade, he was occasionally leading Socratic Circles in class. He joined the basketball team, where he used his social capital to positively influence teammates by showing them that it was OK for sports jocks to also care about academic achievement.

Sephun now facilitates restorative practices workshops with Dominique, during which he explores the boundaries of his own leadership skills. In one workshop, a high school teacher asked the group for advice on increasing academic rigor while at the same time improving and deepening relationships with students. Sephun responded as follows: "I don't have any advice for you. I'm just a kid. But I want to thank you for being the kind of teacher who wants to be better and to push kids to be better. I go to a school where all my teachers are like that. Your kids are lucky to have you."

2 | Relationships and Meaningful Instruction: The Foundations of Restorative Practices

Jeremy scrambles off the bus each day because he likes to be the first one to arrive at his 2nd grade classroom. It wasn't always that way. His mother recalls not too long ago, when the start of every school day morning was a battle.

"I'd do everything to get him moving toward school," she says. "I'd make his favorite breakfast, promise him a treat after school, and when that didn't work I'd yell at him. I had no idea what he was facing."

Jeremy is fortunate: his elementary school focuses on restorative practices. Through problem-solving discussions with his family, teacher, and several other caring adults, the school learned that he had difficulty with several other boys in his class and that the deteriorating relationships were taking a toll on him. Jeremy wasn't being bullied, and he wasn't always in the right himself, but he needed help repairing relationships with some of his classmates. Jeremy's teacher realized that by employing more explicit social and emotional learning opportunities in her classroom, she could promote healthier relationships with all of her students. Of all the interventions she implemented, setting aside a few minutes to talk with Jeremy each morning may well have been the most important. It wasn't the content of the conversations that mattered; it was the fact that his teacher made him feel valued.

An Invitation to Learn

Purkey and Stanley (1991) raise the question: *How do we invite students into learning?* When we invite students into learning, we engage in what the authors call "invitational education" (p. 13), which they contend rests on the following four elements:

1. **Trust** that the environment will remain safe and consistent. This means that adults and students both are good to their word and held accountable to it. In a trusting environment, we strive to be our best selves each day, but we don't live in fear that we'll be ostracized on days when we are less so.

2. **Respect** that is mutual and unconditional, even when members of the school community are not at their best. Respect is a fundamental belief in the dignity of every person, regardless of age or role. As educators, we're attuned to the use of language, and we worry when people say that they "demand respect" from others. When you show respect, it in turn is shown to you.

3. **Optimism,** which is at the core of why we all go to work every day. We believe that our students can learn and that communicating that belief will result in their progress. Optimism is grounded in a realistic (but not cynical) view of circumstances.

4. **Intentionality**—the key to turning optimism into results. Simply believing in something won't make it come true—you have to act upon it. We teach, we intervene, we reteach, we assess progress, and then we teach again. Being intentional means that we consciously implement sound practices that get results.

We can all agree that these qualities contribute to building positive relationships with students. And yet, schools are filled with students who avoid contact with their teachers. Why? We suppose the short answer is that schools are filled with human beings. Purkey and Stanley (1991) describe four distinct types of teachers (see Figure 2.1):

2.1 Four Teacher Types

Intentionally Uninviting	Intentionally Inviting
• Dismissive • Alienating • Harsh • Vindictive	• Consistently positive • Growth mindset • Purposeful • Sensitive to student needs and takes appropriate action
Unintentionally Uninviting	**Unintentionally Inviting**
• Negative • Low expectations • Low sense of efficacy • Pessimistic	• Energetic but unaware • Enthusiastic but naïve • Positive but inconsistent • Laissez-faire attitude

1. **Intentionally uninviting:** These are the teachers who actively belittle children and make them feel small and inadequate. There usually aren't too many of them in any given school.

2. **Unintentionally uninviting:** These are the teachers who aren't sure why students avoid them and don't like their classes. They have a sense of hopelessness about the future, and they keep their expectations low because they don't want to be disappointed.

3. **Unintentionally inviting:** These teachers generally have positive relationships with most students and are reasonably enthusiastic about what they do. However, they're not sure why they make the decisions they do. One problem with being unintentionally inviting is that, sooner or later, you'll be confronted with a difficult

decision about a student and will not know how to react. Teachers in this category will often become aware that they're being unintentionally inviting but will not have the insight necessary to correct their behavior.

4. **Intentionally inviting:** These are the ideal teachers: proactive, systematic, and transparent. They treat all students with respect, build trust with students, have an optimistic outlook, and, most importantly, accomplish these things with *intentionality.* When the efforts of a school are channeled into becoming intentionally inviting to students, families, community members, and colleagues, results can be seismic. Though we believe in the influence of the individual, we know the power of the team. A school that welcomes all with open arms can profoundly affect the school climate.

Building Trusting Relationships

Whereas traditional discipline focuses on the violation of *rules*, restorative practices focus on the violation of *people and relationships.* In every classroom, relationships among individuals are either facilitating students' learning or preventing it. Restorative practices are built on the positive relationships that adults foster with students and with each other in schools. When students care about the relationships they have with others, they work to keep those relationships healthy and to repair any damage to them.

Knowing Students' Names

There are many strategies that teachers can use to foster, build, maintain, and strengthen their relationships with students. First and foremost, however, is one that we tend to take for granted: *knowing students' names.* It can be hard, especially at the start of the year, for teachers to learn all of their students' names, but it is vital that they do so, as this communicates value and importance. Consider Sandra Cisneros's (1991) description of Salvador in her story "Salvador, Late or Early":

Salvador with eyes the color of caterpillar, Salvador of the crooked hair and crooked teeth, Salvador whose name the teacher cannot remember, is a boy who is no one's friend, runs along somewhere in that vague direction where homes are the color of bad weather, lives behind a raw wood doorway, shakes the sleepy brothers awake, ties their shoes, combs their hair with water, feeds them milk and corn flakes from a tin cup in the dim dark of the morning. (p. 10)

Poor, friendless Salvador is clearly not important enough for the teacher to know his name. We can all imagine how much he'll end up achieving in life—and how different his fortunes could be if his teacher only got to know him.

Salvador is fictional, but Joseph Assof (pronounced *ace-off*) is not. Mr. Assof is a high school math teacher. On the first day of school every year, he tells his students that he will know all of their names by the end of the first week—and that if there are any names he can't remember, those lucky students are free to pronounce his name any way they want. It's never come to that, though, because Mr. Assof always remembers everyone's names—and his students respect him for that. Though he will have to do a lot to maintain the relationships that he initiates every year with his opening bet, his efforts at learning students' names communicate to them that he values and understands them as individuals. As Qualia and Corso (2014) note, students can usually tell that adults who use fillers such as *sweetie, honey,* or *sir* have probably forgotten their names—and they expect that those who care about them will remember.

Bringing the Right Attitude to School

In addition to knowing students' names, teachers must choose what attitude they'll bring with them to school each day. Students can tell when the adults around them are in a bad mood. When they notice snide comments and sarcasm, their observations risk damaging the trust they place in us. That doesn't mean we should avoid conversations about our sorrows and joys; sharing personal information, as long as it isn't confidential, is a great way of building relationships. The harm lies in exhibiting a poor attitude for no discernible reason. Of course there is pain in each of our lives. As we write this, Nancy's mom is having major surgery, so she is consumed with worry—but when she shows up to work, she chooses the attitude that she will display for the learners in front of her. Given that we work at a health-focused high school, Nancy is able to talk about the issues her mom faces with several students during passing period and lunch. She doesn't hide her worry from her students, and she lets them know that she is going to be gone from school for several days to help with the recovery period. We are not asking educators to shut all their emotions away but, rather, to carefully frame their attitudes and attendant behaviors every time they interact with students.

your attitude matters

Getting to Know Your Students' Interests

It is vital for teachers to get to know their students beyond their academic profile. To this end, we encourage teachers to ask students about their interests, hobbies, aspirations, and family lives. When we humanize one another, it's much harder to be harsh, rude, or defiant. Figure 2.2 shows a simple student interest survey that you can use to better understand your students. One 3rd grade teacher we know, Max Andrews, uses this survey with great success. Periodically, over the course of the year, he meets with students and asks them to update their entries on the survey. He then provides the surveys to the students' 4th grade teachers, so they can have a sense of each individual student.

Teachers can also use information gleaned from the survey to make connections with individual students during lessons. For example, when Mr. Andrews's students were studying biomes and life-forms in diverse climates and environments, he remembered that Amal had

2.2 Student Interest Survey

1. When people want to know about _____, they ask you.

2. When you have an hour of time to yourself, and you don't have to do chores or homework, what do you like to do?

3. Imagine you have one week to travel for free anywhere in the world. Where would you go, and what would you do while you were there?

4. Let's say you have a time machine. What time and place in history would you choose to visit, and why?

5. If you had $25 to spend on anything, what would it be, and why?

6. What do you hope we do this year in our classroom?

7. Please rank yourself on a scale of 1 (I need lots of help) to 10 (this is a personal strength) on the following academic skills. This will help me be a better teacher for you.

   _____ Spelling

   _____ Reading assignments

   _____ Grammar

   _____ Researching a topic

   _____ Writing about experiences

   _____ Working in a group

   _____ Writing about information

   _____ Leading a group

   _____ Argumentation writing

   _____Working independently

   _____Class discussions

   _____Presentations

8. Last question: If someone wrote a book about your life, what would the title be?

previously lived in the desert and invited her to share what she knew about life-forms there. Mr. Andrews also recalled that Hector had visited Florida and was very excited to talk about the swamp tour that he went on with his grandparents, so he asked him to share as well.

Asking students to share their knowledge in this way communicates to them that they are valued as individuals. In our years listening to students share in class, we have learned of divorces, marriages, deaths, births of new siblings, threats to personal safety, homelessness, and a host of other things that have improved our relationships with students.

Students of all ages have experiences that shape them, and knowing what they are helps teachers develop strong relationships and effective learning environments. Take, for example, 2nd grade teacher Monica Stewart. Her students were a wonderfully diverse mix, and she regularly integrated their interests and personal experiences into class discussions. However, one student troubled her. Afia refused to participate in groups, did not complete assignments, and often tore up papers that Ms. Stewart would give her. She also said rude things both to her classmates and to her teacher. But Ms. Stewart did not give up on Afia—in fact, she resolved to meet with Afia weekly to try getting to know her better. No one at school really knew Afia, and the meeting Ms. Stewart held with her parents at the start of the school year was not especially revealing.

Over several weeks, Afia began to trust Ms. Stewart. Eventually, she disclosed the horrors of war and brutality that she had witnessed in her home country of Pakistan—including the killing of her brother. Ms. Stewart took the opportunity to connect Afia with the school counselor, who in turn got her enrolled in long-term counseling. It became clear that Afia had post-traumatic stress disorder and a great deal of survivor's guilt. When Afia's mom heard from the school about Afia's disclosures, she was surprised that her daughter even remembered what had occurred and gladly agreed to enrolling her in counseling.

Most of the time, the information teachers gain from talking with students is not as dramatic and life-changing as Afia's—but when it is, it really matters. We believe that all behavior is a form of communication: students are trying to tell us something with their actions that they may not have the words to say another way. In essence, students engage in problematic behavior either to get something or to avoid something. When we understand that, we can work to figure things out and get students on the right path.

Home Visits *can we do this?*

Sometimes, getting students on the right path involves a home visit. Home visits allow teachers to talk with families on their own turf and build relationships with parents while furthering their relationships with students. When asked about the benefits of home visits, teachers have reported several positive effects, including "beneficial relationships and better communication with parents, more appreciation of the influence of the child's home environment related to school performance, and a better understanding [of] the child's behavior in school" (Meyer, Mann, & Becker, 2011, p. 191). Home visits can also help teachers to address any cultural gaps that may affect students' behaviors or learning in school.

The California-based Parent/Teacher Home Visit Project has developed best practices for launching a sustainable home-visit program, including the following suggestions:

- Make visits voluntary for educators and parents, but seek at least 50 percent participation from a school's staff.
- Compensate educators for their home-visit work, and train them effectively.
- Always send educators out in pairs.

- Visit a cross-section of students—ideally all of them—rather than target any particular group.
- Focus the visits on building relationships. (Hynes, 2014, p. 49)

Doug's first home visit ever was to a 9th grader who was disengaged from school. Mario was absent more than half the time, and when he did attend school, he didn't contribute much in class. He was failing all of his classes and was likely to have to repeat the grade, which would have put him at great risk of eventually dropping out of school completely.

The school social worker, Raphael, asked Doug to come along with him on a visit to Mario's home. When Doug and Raphael arrived, Mario's mom asked them to take off their shoes and come inside, where she served them some spicy black bean soup. The three of them talked for a while, mostly about Mario. "I don't know what to do," said his mom. "He just won't get up. He says that he doesn't care if he fails. But we didn't come here for that."

About 25 minutes into the visit, Mario came home. He entered the kitchen, calling for his mom. Doug and Raphael had told him that they would visit, but apparently he didn't believe it because he came to an abrupt halt when he saw them. Staring in disbelief, he said, "Really? You came to my house? And you're eating Mom's soup?" Not knowing what else to say, Doug said, "Yeah, and it's really good. I'm going to come for soup every day that you miss school. We all care about you. We want you to graduate more than you do. But someday, you'll want it just as much as we do." His mom started crying, and Mario said, "See what you did? Now she's crying."

Raphael responded, "Yeah, moms cry. But do you want her crying as you walk across that graduation stage or because you've dropped out and aren't doing anything with your life? We're here to help you, man. You can do this. We believe in you."

At this, Mario started crying too and promised to try harder. It wasn't easy, and there were certainly setbacks, but that home visit was the first step on the path to Mario's graduation and his eventual entry into the Army, where he proudly serves his country. To paraphrase Bronfenbrenner (1979), every child needs at least one person who is crazy about him or her. Mario just needed a couple of adults.

Extracurricular Activities

Attending extracurricular events sends a powerful message that student interests are important. Nancy has attended a number of elementary school student performances, dances, and music recitals, and every time she does, students tell her the next day that they saw her in the audience. Not only does Nancy enjoy seeing current and former students, but she also knows that the time she spends doing so is a good investment in relationship building. Similarly, Dominique doesn't miss a middle or high school sporting event, where he likes to start conversations with students and families.

Here's an example of how extracurricular activities can help foster positive relationships with students. Although Savannah didn't present any problematic behaviors in her 7th grade class, she didn't seem to have many friends and was often alone. Her teachers regularly invited her to join groups at lunch and other social events, but she would always decline. (As an aside, having lunch with students on a regular basis is a great way to build relationships—students are often shocked that their teachers eat at all, let alone alongside them! At our school, we purposefully did not create a staff lunchroom so that teachers would have the opportunity to eat lunch with students.) Each week, Savannah's school let students know about local activities that might interest them, such as guitar lessons or football tryouts. One week, Savannah heard that the YMCA was offering a water aerobics class. On the day of the class, she showed up with a signed permission form and seemed like an entirely different person: she was helpful, engaged, and attentive to her peers. She even reached out to the teacher who had first brought the class to the school's attention, suggesting to her ways that they might better prepare students for the class. Over the next couple of weeks, the teacher got to know Savannah and took much of her advice to heart. Although she wasn't one of Savannah's teachers at school, she ended up making a big difference in her life.

On superintendent Joel Pedersen's blog (https://joelped33.word press.com), he argues that every student needs just a single person to care for him or her in order for his or her life to change forever. He even created the hashtag #oneperson to spread the idea. We appreciate the advice that Pedersen offers on his blog, including the following exercise:

1. Hang a picture of every student in your building in the gym.
2. Leave space under each student's picture for staff to write down anything personal (but not private) that they know about him or her.
3. After staff members have made their contributions, start a dialogue with them. What do you notice about what you know about each student? Is every student in a supportive relationship with at least one adult at school?
4. Create a shared plan to make sure that every student has at least #oneperson on staff with whom he or she feels a connection.
5. Be that #oneperson for a student.

As the saying goes, "To the world you may be one person; but to one person you may be the world." Or as Piglet says of love in *Winnie-the-Pooh,* "You don't spell it . . . you feel it." Students know when they are loved and can tell when they're just being tolerated.

Quality, Meaningful Instruction

Relationships are critical, but they only go so far. Just because students feel valued and important doesn't necessarily mean that they will behave in class, especially if instruction is boring or ineffective.

"it doesn't matter how nice you are if your instruction is boring..."

When students have positive relationships with their teachers, they are willing to try paying attention out of respect for their teachers. But if instruction isn't engaging, they are still at risk of misbehaving—whereas if lessons are highly engaging and relevant to students' lives, students will behave regardless of the quality of the student-teacher relationships. Ideally, of course, relationships among teachers and students are strong and instruction is highly effective.

Formative Assessments

Formative assessments can prevent students from becoming frustrated and acting out, especially when they know that the teacher will reteach lessons based on the results. We remember one student, Jose, pouting and throwing down his 9th grade science journal after failing an assessment. Jose's teacher reminded the class that they would be revisiting the lessons over the next few days, with a focus on areas that they did not do well on in the assessment. Upon hearing this, Jose perked up, picked up his notebook, and raised his hand. "So you're not gonna put this one in the grade book yet?" he asked. "So I can fix it before my dad gets the e-mail for my grades and thinks I'm stupid?" As this anecdote shows, there is a clear link between formative assessment and student behavior.

Gradual Release of Responsibility

In an effort to improve student learning and classroom environments, we have updated and revised the components of the gradual release of responsibility (GRR) model in our own Framework for Intentional and Targeted Teaching (Fisher & Frey, 2014). By intentionally sharing responsibility with students at different points in a lesson, teachers can monitor student learning and adjust their instruction accordingly. Our Framework for Intentional and Targeted Teaching encourages students who are engaging in GRR to collaborate with their peers using academic language. In addition, GRR requires teacher modeling of both content knowledge and social and behavior expectations, guided instruction designed to address gaps in students' understanding, and independent learning tasks that allow students to try out what they have learned.

Purposeful Learning

For purposeful learning to occur, students need relevant learning targets. When students know what they are expected to learn, why they are expected to learn it, and how they can demonstrate what they've learned, they pay closer attention to their work and engage in less misbehavior.

Here's an example. Students in Ms. Herrera's kindergarten class were rereading the book *The Day the Crayons Quit* (Daywalt, 2013). To invite them into the lesson, Ms. Herrera made the following announcement: "Today, we get to reread our new book, *The Day the Crayons Quit*. But this time, we're going to figure out how Duncan responded to the letters. We already analyzed the text to figure out what each crayon wanted, right? Who remembers what a crayon was complaining about?"

"The red crayon is tired because he has to work on the holidays, like drawing hearts for Valentine's Days," responded Elvida. "And the gray crayon has too much work because he has to draw too many big things, like hippopotamuses and elephants," said Dinello. "Not green crayon," Aisha said. "He doesn't have any problems. He likes to color things green." After several more students had discussed the issues facing the different crayons, Ms. Herrera interjected.

"You all really know this book well," she said. "And remember, today we're going to figure out how Duncan responds to the various complaints. Remember, we're always looking for evidence to add to our responses. And where does the evidence come from?"

In unison the students responded, "From the book!" Tomás added, "It can be the words or the pictures. And we say 'because' to tell people that we have evidence."

"So, let's read this book again," said Ms. Herrera, "but this time we'll be looking for evidence of how Duncan responds to the issues that each crayon raises. When we have finished reading and collecting evidence, we will each write a letter back to a crayon letting it know whether or not Duncan has solved its problem. If the answer is yes, we can describe how Duncan solved the problem in the letter. Isn't that good practice? To write letters when we can help resolve a problem?"

The few minutes that Ms. Herrera spent introducing the lesson prepared her students by inviting them into an engaging learning experience. Because the students were invested in figuring out how Duncan responded to the crayons, they paid close attention to the text—and, in so doing, did not misbehave. The lesson was interesting and relevant, so students did what Ms. Herrera asked of them.

We've come to believe that purpose-driven instruction is a student rights issue: we think that students have the fundamental right to know what they're expected to learn, why they're expected to learn it, and how they will be expected to demonstrate their understanding. It's not sufficient to simply write these beliefs on the board and leave them there; they should drive the learning experience for students and teachers. In addition to helping improve student achievement, clear learning targets are likely to garner student interest, thus focusing their attention on the lesson rather than any potential misbehavior.

Consider the following two sample statements for guiding student learning:

1. SWBAT calculate and graph exponential decay over time.

2. The U.S. Tennis Association has rules about bounce, called rebound. The ball has to bounce to a certain height, and not too much more or less, to be considered a fair ball. Today, we're going to focus on the height of each bounce, counting one bounce, then two, three, and so on. We'll then graph our data to determine whether the decay is linear or exponential. By the end of the class, you'll be able to summarize the change decay (in this case, loss of bounce) over time.

We find the second statement to be way more interesting than the first, and we think that students would, too. By intentionally inviting students to learn about the subject matter, the second statement is bound to pique student interest in the lesson. It's true that the second statement took longer to craft. But if it results in significantly better student learning and less time spent refocusing the class and correcting student behaviors, then the investment is worth it.

[handwritten marginalia: rethinking daily objectives]

There are times when learning targets are too complex and students end up giving up on the lesson. Conversely, there are times when learning targets are too easily achieved and students become bored by the lesson. Giving up and becoming bored can take the same form in class—namely, disruption. For this reason, it is important to take care when devising a relevant purpose for the learning at hand and composing lesson targets for students.

[handwritten marginalia: zone of proximal development]

Collaborative Learning

Research shows that students like school better, have more fun, and learn more when they have opportunities to engage in meaningful interactions with their peers (City, 2014). According to Danielson (2007), "Students assume considerable responsibility for the success of the discussion, initiating topics and making unsolicited contributions" in distinguished teachers' classrooms (p. 82). In part, this is because "a teacher's skill in questioning and in leading discussions makes a powerful contribution to student learning and is valuable for many instructional purposes: exploring new concepts, eliciting evidence of student understanding, and promoting deeper student engagement" (p. 79).

Creating a classroom driven by discussion rather than distraction requires thoughtful planning and well-honed procedures. We have found the following six considerations to be especially important for creating classrooms in which student-to-student interactions prevail.

1. Meaningful and complex tasks. It almost goes without saying, but students need to understand the purpose of the task on which they're working. If they don't, they'll probably lose interest and talk about other things. Importantly, the purpose of an assignment should never be merely to complete it but, rather, to learn something. Tasks should be relevant to students, and students should know exactly how their assignments relate to their learning goals. Tasks should also be sufficiently complex to garner students' attention and effort. Complex tasks invite students to talk with each other more often, trying to figure out how to solve the challenge at hand.

WHY am I doing this?

NOT JUST COMPLETION

productive conversation

In Jeff Bonine's 10th grade biology class, students pair up to complete a word sort identifying the relationships among different vocabulary terms. As they struggle through the task, Mr. Bonine supplies additional information, such as the meaning of *autotroph* and *heterotroph,* to keep students focused on the task.

2. Joint attention to tasks and materials. When students work collaboratively, it's important to monitor both their verbal and non-verbal interactions—the ways in which they point, lean in, hold their bodies, and stick together. These behavioral cues tell us that students are interacting well. To teach students how to interact properly, teachers can use video clips of students modeling the expected behaviors. When showing such clips, teachers should pause and replay the video at significant moments and discuss the value of the observed behaviors. Over time and with practice, students will begin

we "speak" w/o speaking

to incorporate the behaviors into their own repertoires. Alternatively, teachers might use a fishbowl strategy by having students observe one another engaging in collaborative conversations and take notes for later discussion.

In Mr. Bonine's class, the students work collaboratively and engage in conversations with their teacher and with each other. Mr. Bonine uses a checklist to outline behavioral expectations and provide students with feedback about how well they've met them (see Figure 2.3).

2.3 Sample Behavioral Expectations Checklist

Did you do the following today?

_____ Maintained eye contact with speakers

_____ Remained focused on the lesson

_____ Regularly leaned into the group rather than backing away

_____ Used facial expressions to convey interest, questioning, or agreement

3. Argumentation, not arguing. Students engaged in highly productive group conversations use their argumentative skills to interact fruitfully with each other: They make claims, offer evidence, seek clarification, offer counterclaims, and reach consensus or identify points of disagreement. They can disagree without being disagreeable, and they can interact in sophisticated ways as they solve problems.

The proper use of argumentation has to be taught. Some teachers use language frames to guide students' use of argumentation. For example, 4th grade teacher Susana Quiroz used the following frames (among others) related to supplying evidence during science so that her students would practice using academic language (Ross, Fisher, & Frey, 2009):

- The evidence I use to support _____ is _____.
- I believe _____ (statement) because _____ (justification).
- I know that _____ is _____ because _____.
- Based on _____, I think _____.
- Based upon _____, my hypothesis is _____.

Other teachers use the accountable talk strategy to teach students about the habits of classroom talk (Michaels et al., 2010). Three expectations frame this approach:

1. Accountability to the learning community as a fully engaged participant,
2. Accountability for using the most accurate information available, and
3. Accountability for using reasoning, logic, and evidence in discussions.

accountability talk

The teacher's role in accountable talk is vital and involves more than simply posing questions. Instead, the teacher acts as facilitator, intentionally using conversational moves that keep the dialogue going. For example, a teacher might mark the conversation for others by saying, "Did everyone hear that comment? Would you mind saying it again so we can talk about your idea more?" (Additional useful conversational moves can be found in Figure 2.4.)

Ms. Jacobs has spent the year fostering productive argumentation in her 10th grade classroom. She often has the students arrange their chairs in a large circle to ensure that the students' full attention is on each speaker and that everyone gets a turn to contribute. For example, Ms. Miller's students sit in a circle to discuss their ideas about social media, providing evidence of their assertions to their peers and to their teacher in keeping with the principles of accountable talk.

4. Language support. In the disability community, there is a saying: "Not being able to speak is not the same as not having anything

2.4 **Sample Conversational Moves for Teachers**

- Can you tell us more?

- Would you say that again?

- Can you give me another example so we can understand?

- I'd like to hear what others are thinking about _____'s comment.

- Take your time. I can see you've got further thoughts about this.

- Why do you think that?

- Where could we find that information you just brought up?

- I'll restate what you just said. Listen to make sure I got it right.

- That's a great question. Let's pose it to the rest of the class. What do *you* think?

to say." This idea reminds us of how important it is to provide all students with the support they need to express their ideas. When students don't know how to frame their ideas linguistically, they stay silent. Support can come in the form of sentence frames, teacher modeling, word walls, audio devices, and collaboration with peers.

Ms. Codrington uses language charts and specifically focuses on vocabulary development with her 2nd grade students. She honors students by showing interest in their responses, using positive non-verbal signals, and speaking in a respectful tone of voice.

5. Group size. Whole-class discussions are often appropriate for a given learning target, but they allow for relatively few students to participate. For this reason, expert teachers use a combination of whole-class and smaller configurations of two to five students. Groups do not need to all be the same size: some students perform better with a single partner, while others work better in a larger group. However, groups over five will often crowd some students out of the discussion or self-divide into smaller groups. It's important to match the group size both to the task at hand and to the needs of students.

alt. sizes while mixing abilities

The best way to form groups, though not perfect, is alternative ranking: Using a recent assessment, teachers rank students in order of performance, cut the list at the midpoint, place the two lists side by side, and create groups that span both lists. For example, in a class of 34 students, the first group might include students ranked 1, 2, 18, and 19; the next group might include students ranked 3, 4, 20, and 21; and the third group might consist only of the students ranked 5 and 22. Using this strategy ensures a great deal of academic diversity in each group. Groups can be re-formed every four to six weeks based on new assessment information that has been collected.

Ms. Jacbox arranges her 6th grade students into pairs, triads, and foursomes. Some students need to be in smaller groups because they have difficulty managing too many social relationships during a discussion. Ms. Miles has purposefully organized her students into groups to maximize their interactions and to ensure that they support one another in accomplishing their tasks.

6. Teacher's role. The teacher has an important role in both whole-class and small-group discussions. As we have noted, carefully listening to students is essential for guiding their future understanding. Rather than simply giving students information, teachers should question, prompt, and cue their thinking. They should also be aware that their comments will either enhance students' senses of self—their self-esteem, agency, and identity—or damage them. As Johnston, Ivey, and Faulkner (2011) note, "The language we use with children influences, among other things, who they think they are, what they think they're doing, the relationships they have with others, the strategic information available to them in the classroom, and the possibilities available to them for thinking about literacy and their own lives" (p. 232).

Ms. Codrington is thoughtful in her interactions with her 2nd graders. She wants to encourage them to keep talking and to take pride in their deepening understanding. She rephrases their responses and validates their questions, and she asks them questions herself as well as providing them with prompts and cues to guide their thinking about the content.

The Relationship Among Academic Learning, Social Learning, and Emotional Learning

The academic life of a school is inexorably linked to the social and emotional climate of the school. Teachers like Mr. Assof, Ms. Jacobs, and Ms. Codrington are able to enact meaningful instruction because they actively invest in the social and emotional development of their students. In turn, students are able to engage in inquiry and productive group work because they know they are psychologically safe to wonder, speculate, take risks, fail, and try again.

The Collaborative for Academic, Social, and Emotional Learning (CASEL) outlines the following five social and emotional competencies necessary for elementary and middle school students and recommends that schools include each of them in their programs:

1. **Self-awareness:** Accurately assessing one's feelings, interests, values, and strengths and maintaining a well-grounded sense of self-confidence

2. **Self-management:** Regulating one's emotions to handle stress, controlling impulses, and persevering in addressing challenges; expressing emotions appropriately; and setting and monitoring progress toward personal and academic goals

3. **Social awareness:** Being able to take the perspective of and empathize with others; recognizing and appreciating individual and group similarities and differences; and recognizing and making the best use of family, school, and community resources

4. **Relationship skills:** Establishing and maintaining healthy and rewarding relationships based on cooperation; resisting

inappropriate social pressure; preventing, managing, and resolving interpersonal conflict; and seeking help when needed

5. **Responsible decision making:** Making decisions based on consideration of ethical standards, safety concerns, appropriate social norms, respect for others, and likely consequences of various actions; applying decision-making skills to academic and social situations; and contributing to the well-being of one's school and community (Payton et al., 2008, p. 6)

CASEL performed a meta-analysis of more than 300 studies of social and emotional learning programs involving nearly 325,000 K–8 students. The findings were astounding: Children with access to social and emotional learning programs had gains averaging 11 to 17 percentile points higher than those who did not. Even better, CASEL found that the programs studied were effectively implemented by school staff rather than outsiders, "suggesting that these interventions can be incorporated into routine educational practice" (Payton et al., 2008, p. 7).

At the heart of what all of us do is a mission to foster every child's social and emotional development, two key elements of which are empathy and self-regulation. The climate we create for students can enhance or inhibit the development of these traits as well as students' academic learning.

[handwritten marginalia: intentional teaching & climate helps promote this healthy development]

Empathy

Empathy is the ability to accurately identify the emotional states of others and respond to them with care and concern. Although our experiences certainly contribute to our development of it, young children are as capable of empathy as anyone else. Everyone has witnessed toddlers comforting other toddlers who are upset. Teachers of young children give them the language with which to name feelings and teach them the desired prosocial actions.

We previously discussed Ms. Herrera's lesson on *The Day the Crayons Quit* to her kindergarten class. To help develop her students' feelings of empathy, Ms. Herrera intentionally spends time asking them questions about the emotional state of the characters ("Why is the beige crayon sad?" "Why is the peach crayon feeling embarrassed?"). Her students study the pictures and listen again to the text to locate evidence of each character's feelings. Ms. Herrera then turns to developing her students' ability to take empathetic action by asking further questions ("What could you do to help the beige crayon?" "Is there something you could do that would end the peach crayon's embarrassment?").

The students at the middle and high school where we work learn about the "helping" curriculum first identified by Sapon-Shevin (1998). Classrooms that follow the helping curriculum feature a poster with the following four questions:

approaches to "helping"

1. Did you ask for help today when you needed it?
2. Did you offer help to another when you recognized that he or she needed it?
3. Did you accept help when it was offered to you?
4. If you declined help, did you do so politely?

When you think about it, adults use these four helping behaviors in their professional and personal lives all the time. However, it takes sophisticated communication skills and highly attuned social and emotional skills to enact them properly. Helping behaviors are among the "soft" skills that require social intelligence and that are as important as "hard" skills such as technical knowledge for mastering content.

The mathematics classroom is a perfect place for students to develop soft skills to match their hard skills. Students in math classes confront academic challenges that can leave them feeling dispirited or frustrated. For that reason, the math department at our school has spearheaded collaborative learning initiatives and collaborative assessments that require students to regularly engage in help-seeking and help-granting behaviors (Frey, Fisher, & Everlove, 2009). Such an approach allows students to practice the kinds of group tasks that will most likely mark their future professional lives while developing their sense of empathy. When students regularly offer and request help to and from others, their capacity to do both is bound to increase.

Beginning in 6th grade, all students at our school collaborate daily for part of their math period to resolve extended problems. Initially, these group efforts take the form of simple games, but over time the tasks become more difficult, requiring students to ask one another for help and to provide it. The process can be a struggle at times, especially in cases where individual students seek to dominate the group and complete the tasks themselves. Such was the case with Josh, an 11th grade top math student who was accustomed to completing the type of work that his group faced on his own with no difficulty. Worse yet, his classmates were all too happy to let him finish the work on their behalf.

Unfortunately for Josh and his group, the structure of the end-of-unit assessment rendered their approach untenable. The test is administered over two days. On the first day, students are presented with a conventional, skills-based math test that they are to complete individually. But on the second day, the test is an extended problem-based learning task that students are to complete collaboratively. They are graded on how well they can work together productively. The final portion of the assessment requires students to provide written self-reflections; these are graded according to their level of reflective thinking, analysis, recognition of the contributions of others, and personal ownership.

Josh failed the first two-day assessment. Although he scored well on the first day, he scored poorly both on the

how we could deal w/ tough parents

group task and on his self-reflection. His parents were outraged and demanded a meeting with his teacher and an administrator. Their reaction was understandable—Josh had never failed a math test before, and his parents felt that the assessment's emphasis on group tasks was unfair. The meeting was difficult, but the discussion shifted when one of us asked the parents about their professional lives. Josh's mother was a surgical nurse, so she understood how critical teamwork can be. "I work with some incredibly talented doctors," she said. "But if anyone came into the surgical theater and tried to run the show alone, the patient would die. Simple as that."

Supported in tough conversations

Josh's math teacher, Heidi Montoay, responded that although her son's group tasks didn't possess the same life-and-death risks that hers did, they nonetheless required him to learn the skills necessary to work with others—and, especially, to know how and when to ask for help. "Josh is always going to be a top math student," said the teacher. "But if he doesn't know how to channel those talents to the mutual benefit of a team or an organization, his world will be needlessly small."

Within the year, Josh had learned to work well in groups and had grown in his ability to be self-reflective. He even discussed his experiences in his college essay. In "My Journey from Arrogance to Humbleness," Josh wrote about his struggle with having to rely on others who didn't know as much as he did:

> In my arrogance, I thought that meant that anyone who didn't know what I knew was inferior to me as far as skills went. I didn't yet appreciate that people on my team knew other things that I didn't know. But they didn't see me as inferior, although they would have been entitled to. It took me time and experience to understand that the person who keeps the group focused on the task, or the person who stops the discussion to ask a quiet member of the group,

"What do you think?" knows how to do something I don't. I learned from my classmates that mathematics isn't only about the numbers, formulas, and algorithms. Without other people who make me stop and consider an idea that had never occurred to me, my own learning is thwarted.

Though Josh never truly came to love the daily collaborative work and assessments in his math classes, he did learn to appreciate that the helping behaviors his teachers insisted that he learn were useful to him. We can only surmise that his family's willingness to support his teachers and use examples from their own lives helped immeasurably. *we need family support*

Self-Regulated Learning

We want and need our students to be able to draw on an internal compass that helps them make sound decisions. A self-regulating child will suppress impulsive behaviors, delay gratification, and think about alternatives to and consequences for his or her actions whether or not an adult is nearby.

Consider all the behavior problems you have faced in your career. How many of them would you chalk up to students' lack of impulse control? How many were due to their inability to think through their actions before committing to them? How many occurred because an adult wasn't close by to stop the students from acting out? When students can't self-regulate, problems are likely to follow.

In order for students to develop self-regulation skills, they need experience making choices. Unfortunately, some schools are in the business of issuing mandates that reduce choice in an effort to curtail misbehavior. The result is often the opposite of the one desired, with misbehavior erupting as soon as a teacher steps out into the hallway. Though we certainly believe that clear and consistent rules and expectations are vital, we also recognize that rules are really mutually held agreements and that their success depends on each individual's ability to abide by them. To be sure, students need to be supervised and kept safe in ways that are developmentally appropriate. But teachers must balance such caution by providing students with lots of experiences making independent decisions so they can accrue the knowledge gained from both success and failure.

Many teachers give their students a voice in constructing rules and expectations for their classroom. This is vital, as it provides students with a sense of ownership that they otherwise might lack. Dominique worked with an experienced 8th grade teacher, Sarah Lester, who was facing difficulties during two of her science class periods. The classroom-management tools Sarah had relied on weren't working, and she sensed that she was becoming increasingly frustrated with her class—that is, she recognized that she was becoming unintentionally uninviting toward her students. Anxious for help, she asked Dominique to facilitate circle discussions during the two difficult class periods. Over the course of these discussions, each class developed its own rules and expectations (see Figures 2.5 and 2.6). Though they may not seem particularly profound, the written directives served as powerful representations of shared agreements—contracts, if you

2.5 Classroom Rules and Expectations: Example 1

Our 3rd Period Community of Learners pledges to

- Learn something new each day.
- Offer and ask for help.
- Use one voice.
- Show mutual respect.
- Avoid interruption.

2.6 Classroom Rules and Expectations: Example 2

4th period agreements:

- Respect for peers and teachers
- Participation helps us all learn
- Help is offered and requested
- One voice makes learning possible

will—and equipped the teacher with a new set of tools: when the class drifted from its stated agreements, she could remind students of them without resorting to shaming or humiliation.

Preschool classrooms provide young children with opportunities to rehearse making choices through imaginative intentional play, with teachers mediating as students collaborate on planning an extended imaginary scenario. For instance, if one child wants to enact rocking a baby doll to sleep and the other one wants to be a monkey, the teacher might intervene to help the students achieve a satisfactory compromise—in this case, suggesting that the monkey serve as the baby's pet. Although this example may seem trivial, the toddlers involved are learning to adjust their desires in order to play cooperatively.

As children grow into the primary grades, they are introduced to group games with clearer rules, such as those that they play during recess. They acquire the skills needed for taking turns, being members of a group, and delaying gratification, all of which strengthen their ability to refrain from acting impulsively. In the intermediate and middle grades, students gain further meaningful opportunities to experience choice by engaging in longer and more complex projects, helping set their own deadlines, and making design decisions. By the time they reach high school, students should be regularly challenged to set long-term goals and craft plans to reach them. For example, we require students at our school to monitor and self-report their short- and long-term academic progress on a weekly basis; to self-assess their attendance levels and degree of participation in academic interventions as well as their sleep, nutrition, and work habits monthly; and to analyze their transcripts each year to gauge whether they are on track for postsecondary life. Our intention is to strengthen students' sense of self-efficacy by having them monitor factors that are within their control. This approach deprives students of that classic excuse for poor achievement, "My teacher just doesn't like me," and shows them that successes are due to effort rather than innate ability. Both of these results are essential for helping students to develop a growth mindset (Yeager & Dweck, 2012). As they move into young adulthood, students will hopefully internalize the habit of monitoring their progress and making corrections as needed.

Student Voices: "They Really Like Me Here"

Deci and Ryan (1985, 2002) note that all people have three innate psychological needs:

1. **Relatedness**—they want to interact with, be connected to, and experience caring for others.
2. **Competence**—they seek to control outcomes and experience mastery.
3. **Autonomy**—they are compelled to be causal agents of their own lives.

Dianna, a 4th grader, taught us a lot about these needs. She moved into the district midyear with a very thick cumulative folder full of discipline referrals, suspensions, and student study team reviews. Her teacher, Mr. Sandoval, decided to assign her the most coveted classroom job: attendance monitor. He thought that the post would help her get to know her peers. It did that—and so much more.

In general, Dianna's behavior was fine. Perhaps she talked a bit too much to others, but she was respectful, completed her tasks, and asked a lot of very good questions. When she had a chance to share at her parent-teacher conference, she said, "They really like me here. Mr. Sandoval trusted me to do attendance. I get to check on everybody who's here and then walk by myself to the office. Nobody trusted me like that before. Really, nobody really liked me before—and Mom, I even have *friends*."

Wiping tears from her eyes, Dianna's mother responded: "I didn't know that you thought people didn't like you. Is that why you acted out? Because you thought your teacher and the other students didn't care about you? Oh, honey, I'm so sorry."

Dianna's appointment as attendance monitor allowed her to feel trusted, and it also gave her a great feeling of competence. We are reminded of a comment that Randy, a new 9th grader, made in explaining his chronic defiance: "I'd rather be bad than stupid. It's less embarrassing." Wow. How many students would rather be seen as bad than stupid? That is to say: how many students who are targeted for behavioral interventions really need instructional support?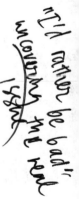

It feels good to learn something. Anyone who has grappled with a thorny problem understands how amazing it feels to figure it out. We want students to feel that same sense of fulfillment, too. We don't want to make learning easy—we want to make it possible. There is a big difference. The instruction students receive should be rigorous and attainable, and students should be given many opportunities to interact with peers as they learn new content.

3 | Classroom Procedures and Expectations: Structures that Support Restorative Practices

Doug and Dominique will sometimes tease Nancy about her tendency to reference the rules and procedures governing any given situation and cite them to justify her decisions. In their words, "Nancy loves a rule." And Nancy doesn't dispute it: rules and procedures help guide her thinking, especially in unfamiliar circumstances. By contrast, Dominique finds rules of a different kind to be especially important: as coach of our school's football team, he relies on a hefty rulebook to ensure that games are conducted fairly and with player safety in mind. For his part, Doug likes to draw on Robert's Rules of Order, a set of parliamentary procedures first developed in the late 19th century, to ensure that all points of view are heard in discussions.

Groups large and small work best with rules and procedures in place as long as they are developed with the people who will be using them in mind. All of us have had experiences where the rules restricted the group's ability to perform. Adherence to rules should never take priority over the well-being of the people involved, but neither is a freewheeling, "anything goes" atmosphere advisable, as such an environment can make children feel scared and uncertain.

Whatever happens each day in a classroom influences the reputation of the school as a whole—for example, an out-of-control classroom contributes to the idea that the entire school is disorderly. But too often, teachers' classroom-management skills are considered individually, without thought to their effect on the larger organization. An unruly classroom doesn't only affect a few dozen people—it affects the entire building and undermines efforts to nurture a more positive climate across the school. *we have to care what other people are doing*

The Value of Rules and Procedures

There is a rich vein of research literature on the importance of safe, orderly, and positive learning environments for the academic and social development of students (e.g., Morgan, Salomon, Plotkin, & Cohen, 2014). Establishing clear rules and procedures to ensure such environments helps educators to facilitate prosocial behaviors among students.

All human societies tend to thrive when they develop rules to structure interactions, ensure fairness, and create a safe climate for all. Our classrooms are no different, and the rules we use with children tend to fall into the same three categories: we structure interactions ("Raise your hand," "Listen as an ally"), ensure fairness ("Take turns," "Show respect for others"), and create a safe climate for all ("Ask for help," "Put materials away when you're finished"). When students are asked about the types of teachers they want, they consistently mention those who "exercise authority without being rigid, threatening, or punitive" (Woolfolk Hoy & Weinstein, 2006, p. 185). Students expect there to be rules; they just want them to be fair.

Effective classroom rules should mirror schoolwide values and be short, positively phrased, a reasonable number, and posted somewhere clearly visible in the room. Although most classrooms do feature rules posters on the walls, they often fade into the overall room design, like the alphabet cards on the wall above the whiteboard. Teachers might discuss the rules with students during the first week of school

we need structure—it just needs to be fair

values are CONCISE

but will rarely invoke them after that—usually because they haven't thought through potentially necessary procedures. Thoughtful teachers think proactively about eventualities and develop procedures to address them. For example, it's hard to imagine any classroom that wouldn't need procedures in place for the following basic situations:

- Entering and exiting the classroom
- Participating in large-group discussions
- Turning in written work
- Managing materials
- Cleaning up
- Obtaining help
- Returning to class after an absence
- Going to the restroom

Well-crafted procedures align to the classroom's rules and to the values of the school. For this reason, we like rules that are broad and simple. The following three are especially appealing to us:

1. Take care of yourself.
2. Take care of each other.
3. Take care of this place.

short, simple, but clear

(See Figure 3.1 for an example of how specific procedures align to these three rules.)

Creating Procedures with Self-Regulation in Mind

As we previously noted, our academic, behavioral, and disciplinary efforts should focus on developing self-regulated learners who have a growing capacity to manage their lives independently. But self-regulation is the product of trial and error—missteps are essential to its refinement. If classroom procedures do not support self-regulation,

3.1 Example of Procedures Aligned to Rules

Rule: Take care of yourself.	Rule: Take care of each other.	Rule: Take care of this place.
Procedures:	Procedures:	Procedures:
• Turning in written work • Obtaining help • Returning after an absence • Leaving to use the restroom	• Entering and exiting the classroom • Participating in large-group discussions • Helping others	• Managing materials • Cleaning up

students leave school with the false belief that their lives are at the mercy of external forces, such as institutions, rather than shaped by their own actions.

[handwritten margin note: teach them that they are in control]

It is important to realistically assess the developmental needs of students before establishing procedures to teach them self-regulatory skills. Younger students will require considerably greater support and supervision than older students, who should be given progressively more room to govern themselves. Unfortunately, procedures at the secondary level are too often no less restrictive than those in the younger grades, suggesting that they are more about power and control than about creating an orderly environment. For example, we can't wrap our heads around the need to demand that young adults ask before going to the restroom. It's humiliating—young people who are about to graduate should be afforded the dignity of managing this matter on their own. We understand that having too many students in the hallways is disruptive, and for that reason we would ask that no more than two students be out of the room at a given time. But why

[handwritten margin note: Bathroom policies...]

can't we let students discreetly choose when they need to step out? Perhaps they could write their names on a whiteboard near the door when they leave, so we know where they are. If any student abuses the privilege, it's worth a conversation, but that's no reason to hold the entire class hostage.

We have a dedicated lecture hall in our school for all senior classes, and there are restrooms nearby for students to use. Classes in the lecture hall last three hours, so students learn to take comfort breaks at judiciously chosen points in the lesson. This is a life skill that we've all used countless times at meetings, conferences, and professional development sessions. The ability to attend to personal needs without compromising the work at hand is paramount. Could you imagine if *you* had to raise your hand and ask permission to use the restroom at work?

Here are some other examples of classroom procedures that teachers use to operate a smooth and orderly classroom:

- A kindergarten teacher plays a two-minute "cleanup" song, to which students respond by singing along and putting their materials away before the song ends.

- A 3rd grade teacher has students immediately store their backpacks in a unit along the back wall as they enter the classroom. Students know that their backpacks belong away from their desks and that they can get materials from their backpacks during transition times.

- A 6th grade teacher has a "we missed you" file for absent students. Each day, an assigned student collects an extra copy of lesson materials, instructions, and notes and places them in the appropriate folder. There is two weeks' worth of material in the file at any given time. Whenever students return from an absence, they know to go to the file to obtain the material they need to catch up.

- A 10th grade teacher uses table tents that have "working" and "ready" printed on either side. Students turn the tents to the appropriate side based on their status. They know that they are supposed to behave differently when they are working than when they are ready for another problem or for the teacher's input. Tents alert the teacher to which groups have completed their tasks. When students at a table turn the card to "ready," the teacher is cued to visit the table and discuss the students' work.

you need these

The standard operating procedures above all provide students with clear expectations. Procedures do not have to be the same from class to class, but when they are, students know what to expect from every educator in the school. Here are a few examples of schoolwide and even districtwide procedures that align with restorative practices:

- In Bakersfield, California, you can go to any elementary or middle school and say "Class, class," and the students and teachers will respond, "Yes, yes," drop what they're doing, and give you their attention.
- At Rosebank Elementary, all students use hand signals to indicate that they can't hear a speaker and to agree or disagree with what is being said. Students are also expected to stand when they answer questions. When they do so, the rest of the class uses hand signals that the teacher monitors to direct the discussion (e.g., "Marco, I see that you disagree. Can you tell us why?").
- At Madison High School, teachers have a procedure in place for getting students to start on a task. After saying, "Give me five," they count down from five to zero, by which time the students know that they must tend to the task at hand.

Teaching and Reteaching Procedures

Once established, rules and supporting procedures need to be taught and, from time to time, retaught. For example, elementary teachers might need to regularly model such tasks as sharpening pencils correctly or joining classroom conversations. Whenever teachers see students forgetting the procedures or challenging their interpretation of them, it's time for reteaching. *misbehavior as a skill deficit : teach.*

The first day back after a long school holiday is a good time to revisit procedures with students. It's also a good time to revise any procedures that no longer suit the students due to changes in the classroom climate. It is wise to schedule periodic checks for understanding of procedures and to ask students for feedback on their efficacy.

The Value of High and Consistent Expectations

In a classic experiment, teachers were given the names of students who, they were told, were likely to do better than their classmates due to their high IQ scores. In truth, the student names had been selected at random. At the end of the study, all the students were tested again, and the results were striking: the students who had been randomly identified as having higher IQ scores all now did, in fact, score higher than their peers (Rosenthal & Jacobson, 1968). Clearly, teacher expectations of what students can achieve make an enormous difference. Over the past five decades, researchers have continued exploring the effects of teacher expectations on student achievement and have found that, though they are modest overall, the effects are more significant and long-lasting for students who are poor, from minority groups, or already struggling as learners (McKown & Weinstein, 2008).

Another study that showed the long-term effects of teacher expectations on achievement tracked 1,000 low-income students from birth to age 15. The students' 1st grade teachers were asked to grade each student's math and reading abilities on a scale of 1–5, with 5 representing the highest proficiency. The researchers then compared these ratings to the students' scores on 1st grade standardized tests. Not surprisingly, the teachers had underestimated the abilities of some students and overestimated those of others. Nine years later, the study revealed that the same students were still being under- and overestimated, suggesting that teacher expectations can have very long lasting results (Sorhagen, 2013).

Ninety percent of teachers report that they have high expectations for all students and that they communicate their expectations effectively, yet only 68 percent of middle schoolers think that their teachers believe they'll make it to college (Carpenter, Flowers, & Mertens, 2004). We communicate our expectations every time we interact with students. When we help students who are struggling, we signal to them that we believe we are spending our time wisely; when we encourage them to enroll in advanced placement courses or strive for honors credits, we signal that we see their potential; when we reaffirm their dreams, we signal that their aspirations have value.

our cues tell students about themselves

When students meet expectations, teachers should have classroom procedures in place to recognize their success. Here's an example. Eighth grade teacher Francisco Reyes ends class each Friday with his students sitting in a circle surrounding a Success Jar. One at a time, students share any academic accomplishments they've experienced that week, which they've also written down on a notecard. After sharing, each student places his or her notecard in the jar. Mr. Reyes uses these notes to plan conversations with students the following week. "When I have a student who isn't being his best self, I pull his note from the Success Jar to remind him of what he did the previous week," he told us. "It's a reminder to both of us, I suppose, about what he is doing to actively engage in his own learning."

We refer to the middle school students at our school as *scholars*. Students are taught the meaning of the word during the first week of school—a learned person, an intellectual. They are addressed as English scholars, health scholars, art scholars, science scholars, history scholars, and math scholars, and throughout the day they hear the language of high expectations. Students each have an individual Scholastic Plan, for which they meet once a quarter with teachers to set goals: improving their grades, making honor roll, clearing any incompletes, and so on.

The teachers at Sunset Cliffs Elementary School have a set of expectations in place called SPARK, which stands for

- Safe,
- Productive,
- Always responsible,
- Respectful, and
- Kind.

These expectations, for which the teachers develop rubrics and indicators, are evident in classrooms, the lunchroom, playgrounds, and even the restroom (where "being responsible" would include washing one's hands and flushing the toilet, for example). Maintaining clear expectations and using the same language schoolwide allows the teachers at Sunset Cliffs to guide students' behaviors and counsel them when they don't meet expectations. As one 1st grade teacher said, "It's just a lot easier to let students know what you expect up front rather than catching them doing something wrong and then making a rule for that. Students deserve to know what we expect and that our expectations for their citizenship are high."

The Value of Teacher Sensitivity

Classroom rules, procedures, and expectations are transmitted to students through a cluster of behaviors known collectively as *teacher sensitivity* (Allen et al., 2013). Behaviors in this category include being responsive to students' learning and emotional needs, caring for students, encouraging students to participate and take academic risks, and comforting students when they need it. Ask students what they most want in a teacher, and the answers will probably reflect these behaviors. In fact, these behaviors are desirable in any relationship: someone who cares about us, challenges us, and comforts us when we are hurting.

[handwritten: what kids need]

Third grade teacher Helena Kitchener begins each school year by asking her students, "What do students want in a teacher?" Together, she and her students craft agreed-upon expectations for what they should expect from her. "It helps me understand what they value and lets them know I will be accountable to them for their expectations," she told us. The class then repeats the process in answer to the question "What does a teacher want in students?" The resulting expectations become the year's Classroom Compact, which is signed by all parties and posted in a place of honor.

Several years ago, the editors of *Educational Leadership* magazine also asked students what they wanted in a teacher (ASCD, 2008). We liked their findings so much that we've used them to frame our discussion about the value of establishing relationship-building procedures.

Students Want Teachers to Take Them Seriously

[handwritten: their problems are REAL to them]

Students don't want to be looked down upon or made to feel as though their problems are insignificant compared to those of adults.

Do you remember how it felt when your heart was broken for the first time and adults chuckled, "It's only puppy love, you'll get over it"? Or the constant reminders from older people that "these are the best days of your life, so you'd better enjoy them"? The struggles of growing up are profound and wrenching. Listen with your heart and offer comfort and encouragement. Remember that these small kindnesses are not forgotten.

they notice

At our school, when teachers have a few minutes free, they stand at one of various locations around the school that feature a sign reading "How can I help you? I have the time," ready to chat with students. Because students know where these locations are, they can drop by during passing period if they'd like. There are no formal requirements associated with this procedure, but teachers are expected to make themselves available on a regular basis. By holding impromptu conversations, adults and students invest in building their relationships with one another.

Students Want Teachers to Challenge Them to Think

challenge them so they know they are capable

Popular notions to the contrary, students *want* to learn—they want to feel as though their time is well spent. When they offer opinions, teachers should ask, "Why do you think that?" If they give brief replies, teachers should prompt them to continue ("Tell me more"). We all appreciate it when our thinking is solicited. It is also important for teachers to provide students with opportunities to investigate issues: because problem-based and project-based learning principles are predicated on a foundation of inquiry, students will often arrive at different solutions, which provides additional incentive for discussion and thoughtful debate.

Pre-algebra teacher Ben Caruthers challenges his students to justify their conclusions and engage in public debate. "I offer my students a difficult math problem almost every day," he told us. "I call it 'You Be the Judge.' It's usually a worked example with an incorrect answer.

I give the students at each table a gavel, then I ask them to speculate as to where the mistake occurred and why; when they think they've got an answer, they bang the gavel and announce, 'Order in the court!' They then share their argument with the rest of us, after which we weigh in with our opinions."

Students Want Teachers to Nurture Their Self-Respect

Few strategies are more effective at improving student behaviors than providing them with leadership roles. Wise teachers actively look for ways to give students responsibility. Elementary teachers often have job assignments in place that rotate each week, such as materials manager or table captain. High school teachers ensure that opportunities to take responsibility abound (selecting books off of a recommended reading list in English, for example, or proposing a research topic in biology class). Giving students "choice and voice" helps them to continually conceptualize who they are as people.

Preschool teacher Ms. Moreno selects a different student to highlight each week as her "kid of the week." The student and his or her family choose a handful of photographs and meaningful objects, which Ms. Moreno then mounts in a shadow box along with facts about the student (e.g., birthday, favorite color, the names of any siblings or pets). The student then shares his or her story with the class and answers any questions. "All children need chances to tell others about themselves, and this gets others asking questions," said Ms. Moreno. "I don't need them to share possessions. I'd much rather have them see that their most valuable possession is themselves."

give space for convos about self

Students Want Teachers to Show Them That They Can Make a Difference

Charitable acts outside the classroom can help to build community among students and teachers. These can take many forms, from random acts of kindness to fund-raising efforts, blood drives, and community activities. In fact, many high schools include community service as a graduation requirement. Students benefit from seeing how their contributions make a difference in the lives of others.

Mr. Harmon's 6th graders use a class wiki to post "help wanted" and "help offered" ads. On any given day, students can check the "help offered" section of the wiki to see who they might turn to for assistance with classwork. If no one is available to help them, they can then post a "help wanted" ad. One student, Sophia, posted the following ad: "Too much to do. Can someone help me prioritize? I just need to talk it through so that I can figure out which assignments to do first." She had a response within an hour from Justine, who replied, "Yeah, I can be your ears. But can you go over the math homework with me?" Sophia and Justine learned that their actions matter and that they can make a difference to their peers.

On a grander scale, the students in Ms. Armstrong's class engage in community service every month, such as providing meals for the homeless and contributing to beach cleanup efforts. The students know that their actions benefit others and that they are important members of the community.

Students Want Teachers to Point Them Toward Their Goals

Letting students establish goals for themselves can propel learning and help them to develop their senses of self. However, students need to understand that goals have three dimensions: mastery, performance, and effort (Alexander & Jetton, 2000). Middle school mathematics teacher Eddie Garza has a procedure in place to help his students establish goals. "At the beginning of each unit, I ask them to fill out a short form that includes the grade they intend to earn [performance], at least two learning goals [mastery], and the time they will devote to accomplishing these goals [effort]," he said. Mr. Garza posts the students' goals in the classroom and meets with individual students briefly each week to check on their progress. "It's shifted the focus of my discussions with students," he said. "Instead of me haranguing them about what they need to do, we can talk about the goals they set for themselves. It promotes ownership, and it's shifted my role from nagging to supporting their goals."

students in control

Students Want Teachers to Make Them Feel Important

Sixth grade teacher Toni O'Leary keeps a board outside her classroom door with the heading "Student in the Spotlight." Each day, she posts a photo of a different student taken in the first week of school along with a short, handwritten description of something the student has accomplished—usually in the form of a contribution to the classroom community, such as offering great ideas during a discussion or assisting a classmate during a task. For Ms. O'Leary, this simple procedure reminds her to recognize individuals and reflect on positive experiences. "It's as good for me as it is for the students," she said. "It reminds me of all the great things that happened during the day."

Students Want Teachers to Build on Their Interests

One measure of how we assess relationships with others is the extent to which they know of and support our interests. Fourth grade teacher Angelina Pawelek asks all her students to complete a "help offered" survey that she designed, on which they are asked to outline areas of interest and expertise, and then posts the results for others to see. If students receive help from classmates, they are asked to leave a comment endorsing them on the posted survey. "I call it Angelina's List," said Ms. Pawelek. "Some students can help with throwing a football; others can help with spelling. I get to know them so much better because they identify their own interests." By establishing a procedure that asks students about their interests and using it regularly throughout the year, Ms. Pawelek has created a channel for building relationships with her students.

these are more than academic

Students Want Teachers to Tap Their Creativity

Sixth grade science teacher Ellen Wainwright posts a weekly "Problem of the Week" on a bulletin board in her classroom, along with piles of sticky notes and pencils for students to use in solving the problem. Problems may be relatively large (e.g., reducing the carbon footprint of our school) or small (e.g., figuring out the best way for the teacher to collect and return student papers). At the end of each week, Ms. Wainwright goes over the students' ideas with the whole class.

"I want to make sure my students see other people's ideas, because these inspire new thoughts," she told us. "I enjoy the fact that I can positively profile students, and I know they enjoy the attention. I'm amazed at how creative they can get!"

Students Want Teachers to Bring Out the Best in Them

It is a given that students will disappoint us and themselves from time to time, some more often than others. We often respond by lecturing students, but that approach is rarely effective. (Nancy's 2nd grade grandson was lectured for disrupting class one day; when his parents later asked him what the teacher had told him, he answered, "I don't know, but it was a lot of sentences.") Better to start by saying to a student, "That's not the [name of student] I know. What's happening?" In this way, we acknowledge the problematic behavior without conflating it with a character flaw and invite the student to lead the conversation.

The Value of Analyzing Problematic Behavior

When problematic behaviors arise, the worst possible time to consider how to respond is in the moment, yet too often that's exactly what happens. We find ourselves reacting in anger and scolding students, who then bury their heads in their arms and remain that way for the rest of the lesson. Or perhaps we choose to ignore the problem altogether because we're tired, it's 2:37 p.m. on a Friday, and we've decided we'll just wait it out and think about it again next week (of course, we never do).

Behavior is how we communicate our wants and needs to the world; we use facial expressions, movement, and words to convey how we are processing all the information that's coming at us. Our students' brains are busy at work determining what they should pay attention to and what they should filter out: "There's sound coming from the hallway—can I ignore it? The teacher is talking and pointing to something on the whiteboard—should I look over there?"

The ABCs of Behavior

As educators, we should seek to recognize *patterns* of behavior so that we can correctly anticipate students' actions. If a student misbehaves in one class but not in another, he or she is waiting for us to notice the pattern. Unfortunately, we are rarely able to devote our full attention to analyzing the behaviors of a single student. It's vital to understand that what happens before and after a given behavior is just as important as the behavior itself. This chain of events is known as the ABCs of behavior: the antecedents to the behavior, the behavior itself, and the consequences of the behavior.

Antecedents are the events that trigger a certain behavior. Sometimes they take time to develop into the behavior: For example, Andrew might get into an altercation at school because he's still angry about an argument he had with his parents the night before. This is known as a slow trigger. Fast triggers are events that occur immediately preceding a certain behavior and as such are usually more apparent than slow triggers: For example, Tomás insults Andrew at the lunch table, and Andrew responds by swearing and taking a swing at Tomás. In this case, the conventional response would be to suspend both students for three days—but what if Andrew is also having a delayed reaction to a fight with his parents at home? Suspension is a woefully inadequate consequence that doesn't get to the root of the conflict (that is, the slow trigger of the student's fight with his parents). Three days later both boys return to school, and nothing is resolved.

Some consequences for behavior are immediate (taking a swing at someone lobbing an insult), and others are delayed (suspending the students involved in a fight). The logic of a consequence isn't always apparent, particularly as it can initially be hard to discern an explanation for the behavior. The conventional approach is to tell students that they "chose" the consequence by misbehaving. However, children and adolescents don't have the same ability as adults to anticipate the ramifications of their behavior. This is especially true in emotionally charged situations.

Keep in mind that consequences shine a spotlight on the intended function of behaviors: we all behave in certain ways either to get something or to avoid something. This is why "cookbook" approaches to behavior management are inadequate and can even cause more harm than good. When we focus on behaviors to the exclusion of their antecedents, we aren't addressing the causes or functions in any meaningful way. Looking for the function of a behavior isn't the same as excusing it or rationalizing it. Rather, establishing the intended function prevents us from identifying consequences that inadvertently reinforce the behavior. If we fail to examine the antecedents of a behavior, we miss the opportunity to locate underlying issues. As Cicero noted more than 2,000 years ago, "The causes of events are ever more interesting than the events themselves."

Let's look again at the example of Andrew. If the function of his behavior is to escape school because he's upset with himself and his parents, then a

[handwritten margin note: Connect consequences to causes]

three-day suspension works to his advantage. But it's possible that Andrew could have escaped his troubles in a less damaging way. A trusted adult might have offered him an emotionally safe space to vent, for example, which could have prevented the eventual fight with Tomás. Even if the fight had not been prevented, the consequences could have been different, perhaps focused more on encouraging restorative practices between the two boys that might equip them both with constructive tools to deal with their frustrations.

Here's a less dramatic example of the ABCs in action. Nancy was in a classroom with a first-year teacher who didn't know how to deal with three 4th grade students who kept getting up from their seats and being disruptive. The students weren't mean-spirited, and their classmates didn't seem bothered by what they were doing, but the teacher was frustrated at having to repeatedly redirect them. The teacher knew that confrontation would likely escalate the situation, but he wasn't sure what he should do. Nancy observed the three boys and noticed that when the content got more challenging, their behavior escalated. Clearly, the *antecedent* to their behavior was the introduction of a more difficult task, and the intended *function* was avoidance. Their skill or performance gap was likely the source of the problem.

After Brian Patterson assigned his class a collaborative task, he and Nancy spoke quietly to the three boys. The teacher made sure to separate the behavior from their character ("This isn't the kind of learner I've come to expect from you") and acknowledge the suspected antecedent ("It seems like you're getting up and roaming around when the task is tougher. Is that true?"). The teacher then offered a solution ("I'm going to make a point of coming to your table first to clarify after I explain the task. That way you can ask as many questions as you need") and some encouragement ("I want you to be successful today, and I know you want to be successful as well. We'll work together to make that happen"). Things didn't miraculously improve as soon as Nancy and the teacher intervened, but the three students behaved noticeably better for the rest of the class period. Later in the day, one of the disruptive students apologized to the teacher for his behaviors.

Developing the habit of trying to discern the intended function of a behavior can provide teachers with a frame for deciding on how to intervene. Figure 3.2 shows a decision-making matrix for determining

3.2 Decision-Making Matrix for Responding to Problematic Behavior

What is the function of this behavior?	Does this warrant immediate intervention? ["Yes" answers indicate that immediate intervention is needed]	Should intervention be delayed or deferred? ["No" answers indicate a possible need to delay the intervention]	What are ways to intervene?
• Social attention • Obtaining something • Avoidance • Escape • Power or control	• Is the misbehavior harmful? • Is the behavior distracting to others? • Is the behavior contagious? • Does the student appear to be testing the system?	• Do I have all the facts? • Is the student in an acceptable state of mind? • Am I in an acceptable state of mind? • Is this an isolated incident?	• Move closer • Signal • Redirect • Replace • Reduce • Relocate • Ignore • Reinforce
Why?	*When?*	*When?*	*How?*

whether behaviors warrant immediate or deferred intervention and possible responses.

Sometimes teachers need to examine ongoing problematic behaviors and see if they can help students to adopt prosocial behaviors instead. In these cases, teachers might use the more formal process of functional behavioral analysis (Alberto & Troutman, 2012). Although a full exploration of functional behavioral analysis is beyond the scope of this book, it's worth noting some useful elements of the process. One such element is the scatterplot (see Figure 3.3), which educators can use to identify patterns related to a behavior. The grid might be divided into 10-, 15-, or 20-minute intervals or even longer ones if the problematic behavior isn't that frequent. Scatterplots are useful for identifying the frequency and the severity of behaviors and can be used to assess the effectiveness of behavior support plans.

One limitation inherent to scatterplots is that they don't provide any information about antecedents or consequences. For that reason, people often combine them with a tool that allows for the documentation of observable behavior (see Figure 3.4). For example, when analyzing the spitting behavior of one of her 1st grade students, a teacher noticed that the student tended to spit at his classmates when they were ignoring him. The teacher decided to focus her efforts on teaching the student how to gain his classmates' attention rather than on punishing him for engaging in the behavior.

It's often useful to ask students directly about their behavior, as they might not realize that it is a cause for concern or might have interesting insights into it. Figure 3.5 shows a sample survey that teachers can use to glean useful information from students about their behavior.

Once teachers have collected sufficient data related to student misbehaviors, they can review the data for patterns and recommendations. If educators aren't sure about the function of a behavior or how best to address it, they might consider employing the following sentence frames:

3.3 Scatterplot Template

Student: _____ Grade: _____

School: _____

Date(s): _____

Observer: _____

Behavior of Concern: _____

Additional Relevant Information: _____

Code Used (if any): _____

Setting or Class	Times or Intervals	Day/ Date	Day/ Date	Day/ Date	Day/ Date	Day/ Date	Total Times Observed

Observation Notes (e.g., specific circumstances under which the behavior occurred, particular antecedents that triggered the behavior, times/conditions during which the behavior did not occur, patterns observed):

_____

_____

_____

Source: Adapted from *Addressing Student Behavior: A Guide for All Educators,* a technical assistance manual prepared by the New Mexico Public Education Department, Quality Assurance Bureau, 2010. Available: http://www. ped.state.nm.us

3.4 Survey of Observable Behavior

Student: _____

Observer: _____

Date: _____

Time Period: _____

Date	Time	What exactly did the student do? Where and with whom?	What was the student doing immediately before the behavior occurred?	Speculate on the communicative intent of the behavior: mood, illness, change, transition, control, discomfort, frustration, etc.	How long did the behavior last?	What was the staff response to the student's behavior?	What was the student's response to the staff?

3.5 Sample Student Survey

We are gathering information in order to better understand what goes on in and out of the classroom, and we need your help to get an accurate picture. Please answer these few questions as openly and honestly as possible.

Q. Do you think that what goes on outside of school affects how students work and behave in class? If so, how? Please provide an example.

A. _____

_____

Q. Is there anything happening in your life outside of school that affects your work and behavior in class?

A. _____

_____

Q. Most students are bothered by someone or something that goes on at school. What bothers you?

A. _____

_____

Q. Have you recently been punished or reprimanded for something you did in school? Please explain what happened.

A. _____

_____

Q. How about [target behavior]? What was going on the last time or other times you behaved that way? What happened just before, or what caused you to behave that way?

A. _____

_____

Q. What usually happens right after you behave or another student behaves contrary to expectations?

A. _____

_____

Q. What do you think was expected of you? Was the consequence fair or not, and why?

A. _____

_____

Q. How do you feel about [specific subject/teacher/student]?

A. _____

_____

Q. How do you think [specific subject/teacher/student] feel(s) about you?

A. _____

_____

Q. What happens when you *do* do exactly as you are expected? What *should* happen?

A. _____

_____

Q. What consequences have you received for [behavior]? What consequence *should* you have received?

A. _____

_____

Q. Can you think of any situations in school that you would really avoid if you could?

A. _____

_____

Q. Can you think of anything that you wish would happen that doesn't happen often or at all?

A. _____

_____

Q. Name one or two things you wish were different at school.

A. _____

_____

Q. Name one or two things you wish were different outside of school.

A. _____

_____

Q. Name one or two things you wish were different about yourself.

A. _____

_____

Source: Adapted from *Addressing Student Behavior: A Guide for All Educators,* a technical assistance manual prepared by the New Mexico Public Education Department, Quality Assurance Bureau, Fall 2010. Available: http://www.ped.state.nm.us

- When the behavior occurs, it is usually in the context of
  _____ and preceded by _____ trigger(s).
- The student's response to the trigger(s) is to _____
  (describe the behavior).
- The result of the behavior is usually _____, which
  serves to _____ (describe the need that the behavior
  meets).
- The function of the behavior is likely to be _____.
- The behavior appears to be a _____ (describe the
  skill deficit or performance deficit) because _____.

One team of middle school teachers used sentence frames to determine how to respond to a student who frequently left the class. Ricardo was allowed to take self-initiated breaks as part of his individualized education plan, but he was abusing the privilege. His teachers' immediate reaction was to discontinue his breaks altogether, but this only led to a wider range of misbehaviors on Ricardo's part, from verbal outbursts to crying under the table to insulting classmates. When the teachers analyzed the problem further, they came to realize that Ricardo needed the breaks but that they had not made their expectations clear to him. They also realized that Ricardo often used the breaks to gain the attention of certain staff members. (Ricardo likes to share the drama in his life with others and often tells the same story over and over.)

As part of their plan, the teachers decided to limit Ricardo's breaks and to schedule time for him to meet with the adults of his choice so that he could talk with them (see Figure 3.6). Within three weeks of implementing the plan, Ricardo was no longer exploiting his breaks from class. He met with the staff member of his choosing each day and had his or her undivided attention. Best of all, his performance in class improved, reducing his stress and his need to talk about getting bad grades.

3.6 Ricardo's Support Plan

Expectation: To remain in the classroom, with the support of two breaks, during all class periods

Cell Phone & iPod Usage: Phone or iPod will be turned in to Ms. Matheson upon arrival to school. If Ricardo does not turn in his phone or iPod, a phone call will be made home, and he will not be allowed to bring the item to school until a meeting is held. Parents will be asked to come to school and collect the device.

Rules for Classroom Breaks:

- Two 5-minute breaks outside of the classroom per class period if needed.
- Ricardo will notify a staff member in the classroom, who will accompany him on his break.
- Staff will model and teach Ricardo how to take an appropriate break. Staff support during break times will decrease gradually over time.
- Ricardo will be encouraged to learn how to take his breaks inside the classroom but will still be permitted to take them outside if he desires.
- If Ricardo wishes to speak with another staff member, he may make an appointment with him or her outside of class.
- Ricardo will be required to meet with a staff member for the first half of lunch if he
     - Leaves the classroom without telling a staff member.
     - Leaves the staff member while on his break.
     - Takes more than three breaks in one period.
- Ricardo will be required to meet with a staff member during lunch for however many minutes he misses class time over his two allotted 5-minute breaks. If he needs to make up more time than is reasonable for lunch, he will meet after school with a staff member.
- It is very important to remember that one of Ricardo's reinforcers is *attention*. Therefore, we must remember that if he is making up time with staff during lunch or after school, we should ensure that the time spent doing so doesn't reinforce his bad behavior. Ricardo should not be interacting with peers or other staff members during this time. Instead, he should be completing any missed work. If he wants to discuss a problem or emotional issue, he needs to do so during a scheduled time. Only discussions pertaining to the completion of missed work and prompts as needed should take place during this time.

Daily Reinforcement: A daily reinforcement will be added to the plan with Ricardo's input.

Staff Expectations: A staff member will be assigned to each of Ricardo's classes every day and available to take breaks with him and join him at lunch if necessary. Assigned staff will monitor and record the number and duration of Ricardo's breaks.

The Value of Understanding Escalation and De-escalation

Perhaps the most important advice that we can offer is to avoid escalating situations whenever possible. All too often, adults become too confrontational and assert their power too forcefully. Wolfgang (2001) suggests that teachers can respond to problematic behaviors along a continuum based on the severity or intensity of the issue:

1. **Looking**—making eye contact or using a simple gesture
2. **Naming**—talking quietly to the student, identifying the problematic behavior
3. **Questioning**—asking the student what he or she should be doing at the moment
4. **Commanding**—informing the student what needs to be done instead of the problematic behavior and may note consequences for not complying
5. **Directing**—the teacher physically preventing the problematic behavior from happening (such as separating students who are fighting)

Some situations require teachers to do very little, while others require them to exert a moderate level of control and power. In these cases, teachers call out the misbehavior, label it problematic, and name their desired replacement behavior. Think back to our earlier example of the three disruptive students in the first-year teacher's class. Had the students' misbehavior persisted after the teacher's initial intervention, the teacher might have intervened a second time to address them in a more commanding manner:

> When you leave your group and interrupt the other groups, you are interfering with their learning. Worse yet, you are not making it possible for your own learning to happen. You need to stay within your own group and signal to me

when you're stuck so that I can give you the help you need. You have my assurance that I will help you, and I need your assurance that you will do the same.

It is important to note that no one type of response is superior to another; rather, they represent a series of measured responses that advance only as the situation warrants. Failure to begin by exerting minimal control and advancing methodically from there can lead to escalation of the misbehavior. If the teacher in our earlier example had asserted a high degree of power and control with his initial intervention, he might well have provoked defiance from students.

start small w/ intervention w/ intervention

Teacher Broc Arnaiz found himself in a difficult situation when he mispronounced a student's name while taking roll for an internship program orientation. The student, a 9th grade boy, reacted angrily, standing up and hurling profanities and insults at Mr. Arnaiz. He was clearly poised for a fight. Mr. Arnaiz responded by apologizing: "I'm not sure what I did wrong, but I can see it was something. I'm sorry I upset you." He did not get into a power struggle with the student, demand that he sit down, or threaten to send him to the principal. The student was taken aback, but only a bit. Mr. Arnaiz sent a quick instant message asking for help from Dominique. When Dominique arrived, he asked the student if they could talk—and the student replied with another volley of insults.

Dominique took the student out into the hallway and asked him what was wrong. "Stupid Americans can never pronounce my name," he said. The two then discussed the importance of teaching people the right way to say a name before expecting it of them. After a while, the student became fed up. "I don't want to go to this stupid school," he said. "I don't want to be a doctor. My mom only made me come here because of my brother."

Dominique asked the student what he really wanted to do and learned that he wanted to be an architect.

"You know, our hospital partners have entire engineering departments," said Dominique. "Do you think you'd be interested in an internship somewhere like that?" Surprised, the student said yes.

"Well, we can ask Mr. Arnaiz to place you there," said Dominique, "but first I think we need to talk with him."

"Yeah, that was bad," said the student. "But he did say my name wrong, and I'm sick of it."

Soon after, Dominique, Mr. Arnaiz, and the student met. The student apologized and explained why he was upset. During their conversation, Mr. Arnaiz said, "I hear you. People say both my first and my last name wrong all the time. I meant you no disrespect, but you hurt my feelings when you said that we were stupid Americans. I was just trying to make sure that you were prepared for your internship so that you didn't show up for it confused and not sure where to go."

In the above example, Mr. Arnaiz used the following techniques that are particularly effective for de-escalating emotionally charged situations:

- Speaking in a soft, low tone
- Acknowledging and naming the student's feelings
- Avoiding sudden movements and labeling one's movements in advance so as not to startle the student
- Keeping hands where the student can see them (but not placing hands on the student)
- Refusing to take the student's outburst and comments personally

Knowing how to de-escalate student behavior is a critical component of classroom management. As the adults in the school, we have to keep our egos out of it and think of how best to normalize a heated situation.

Student Voices: "The Rules Are the Rules, but You Can Get Another Chance"

Middle school student Jorge arrived at school one day wearing a shirt that read "Tequila makes me do bad things." The shirt clearly violated the school dress code, which had been communicated to him clearly and often. The dress code read, "Ask yourself this question: Does what you wear communicate respect for yourself and the learning environment?"

In some schools, teachers ask students whose shirts violate the dress code to turn the shirts inside out. When this happens, the students' peers often notice and think they've put their clothes on backward. Fear of such humiliation leads some students to refuse to turn their shirts inside out. Jorge's school took a different tack. An administrator told him that he could have a school pride shirt in exchange for the tequila shirt. Somewhat reluctantly, Jorge agreed. "I just have to ask your mom if it's OK," said the administrator. "Can you call her really quick so that you're not late for class? You're not in trouble, but I want to be sure she agrees to the trade." When Jorge's mom heard about the offensive shirt, she was embarrassed. "I had no idea that he even had that shirt," she said to the administrator. "Yes, of course, make the trade. And you can burn that shirt when you get your hands on it."

Later in the day, the administrator overheard Jorge telling his friends how he got the cool new shirt he was wearing.

"Yeah, like, I coulda got in a lot of trouble because I made a bad choice," he said. "But [the administrator] just told me again what the expectations are and then made sure I could live up to them. You gotta respect that. The rules are the rules, but you can get another chance."

4 | Peace Building: Using Informal Restorative Practices Every Day

It's hard to forget the ones we lose. Several years ago, before we knew about restorative practices, a 10th grade student we'll call Phillip enrolled in our school. From the first day, he made his presence known: He was profane and hostile, and he used his physical stature to intimidate others. Although never physically violent with us, he clearly communicated his disdain for school and every adult in it. Uncooperative in class, he quickly developed a reputation among students as someone to avoid. Administrators responded in the usual ways, by turns cajoling him, bargaining with him, isolating him, and suspending him. Nothing worked. A parent meeting with Phillip's father ended disastrously, suggesting that Phillip's behavior reflected his upbringing. Within six months, Phillip had withdrawn from the school because the family moved to a new apartment. Frankly, we all breathed a sigh of relief.

But Doug stayed in contact with Phillip, who had a bumpy academic road: he was suspended regularly and transferred a few times, but he managed to stay in school and graduate. Phillip admitted to Doug that he had made his own life more difficult, especially by using alcohol and drugs, but that he'd managed to overcome these hurdles. After Phillip graduated, Doug asked him how he thought he'd succeeded in making it through school.

"I don't know," Phillip replied. "I guess they just didn't give up on me."

At our school, we did give up on Phillip. We used the approaches that we knew at the time, and when they didn't work, we turned to punishment. When Phillip pushed us away with his misbehavior, we responded by distancing ourselves. We didn't have the capacity at the time to build solid relationships with a wary adolescent who had learned early on not to trust adults. When Phillip violated school or classroom expectations, we answered with suspension, as if that would somehow "teach him a lesson." We used that phrase a lot: *teach him a lesson*. We wanted Phillip to be contrite, but we never taught him how to move from regret ("I'm sorry I got caught") to remorse ("I'm sorry I caused harm") to making amends ("I want to repair the damage I caused") to true contrition ("I want to be a better person"). No one learns to be a better person by spending a few days suspended from school. At best, suspending students can cause them only to regret what they've done. In retrospect, the suspensions we imposed were more about vengeance than instruction. We were being intentionally uninviting

*we have to teach this process:
REGRET →
REMORSE →
AMENDS →
CONTRITION →*

If Phillip were to enroll in our school today, our response to him would be totally different. At the beginning of each year, we ask teachers to flag students who might need special attention and add their names to a "high flyer" list, and Phillip would clearly be on that list. We would have identified an adult in the school to build a relationship with him and serve as an advocate. Other staff would have sought to establish relationships with him as well, to build trust. One way to build trust is by employing the 2 × 10 strategy: spend 2 minutes talking with a student about anything other than school for 10 consecutive days. This simple strategy has positively affected hundreds of students in our school and in schools around the world.

Phillip's teachers would receive better support today, too. When he was enrolled with us, Phillip experienced a patchwork quilt of classroom-management practices that changed with every class.

Back then we paid little attention to the importance of developing a consistent set of practices. More important, we didn't have restorative practices in place, so our procedures were about adjudicating conflict rather than fostering social and emotional growth. Although teachers can certainly benefit from using restorative practices in their individual classrooms, they are best implemented consistently throughout the school—a major undertaking.

Keeping, Making, and Building the Peace

The climate of any school reflects three main practices for preventing and managing conflict: peacekeeping, peacemaking, and peace building (Bickmore, 2011). Differences in the extent to and efficacy with which these practices are implemented from school to school can account for dramatically contrasting school climates. Schools that lean heavily toward peacekeeping tend to have security measures in place and seek to control and limit student freedoms to maintain order. But schools don't need metal detectors to value peacekeeping; many classroom rules and procedures are designed to ensure safety. By contrast, peacemaking practices focus on dialogue and conflict resolution, especially through forums that purposefully lead students to a greater understanding of themselves and others. In cases where students harm others, peacemaking approaches value restoration and restitution over punishment. The third main type of practice, peace building, refers to investments in prosocial means of preventing and addressing disputes. _BUILDING- prevention_

Schools that are more invested in peacemaking and peace building than peacekeeping seek to transform their efforts by making them part of the explicit, rather than hidden, curriculum (Bickmore, 2011). Peacemaking efforts include the formal restorative practices of problem-solving circles, victim-offender dialogue, and high-stakes conferences (Costello, Wachtel, & Wachtel, 2010). Peace-building efforts are folded into lessons such that students develop a vocabulary for discussing their perspectives and considering the viewpoints of others. Among staff, the ability to use language that helps others build identity and agency is particularly valued, as is the work of equipping children with the tools they need to resolve conflicts.

You need the vocabulary for how to do this right.

Developing a Restorative Mindset

fairness is a charged topic

Developing a restorative mindset is more complex and personal than some might think. Beliefs about discipline are bound in our own experiences as children, educators, and parents. Discipline is informed by our sense of fairness, which we develop at a very early age: studies show that children as young as 15 months old can detect when food is not equally distributed to others (Schmidt & Sommerville, 2011). Although our beliefs about fairness mature over the years, we're never too far removed from the small child who wails, "It's not fair!" When students violate our expectations, we sense unfairness.

As educators, we also bring our own beliefs about control to bear on our approaches to discipline. Whereas some teachers hold that children are inherently good and will behave under the right conditions, others believe that students will naturally avoid work whenever possible and need to be constantly contained and redirected. Restorative practices can challenge such deeply rooted beliefs by asking us to shift our focus from rules to relationships. We must let go of the idea that accountability equals punishment (i.e., "teach him a lesson") and instead help students progress from acting out to remorse and repair (i.e., "I'm sorry, and I want to make amends").

Challenging our values & subconscious beliefs

Empowerment is at the center of restorative practices, as evidenced in the principle that all parties involved in a conflict must contribute to its resolution—victims, offenders, and anyone else even indirectly affected by it. Students need to be taught and given opportunities to use their problem-solving skills. It would be a mistake to wait for conflicts to arise before enacting restorative practices—that's what we did early on, and it was a mistake.

The International Institute for Restorative Practices identifies a continuum of practices ranging from informal to formal (Costello et al., 2010). In this chapter, we'll be focusing on the following first four informal practices:

1. *Affective statements and questions* that develop a child's sense of agency and identity
2. *Classroom meetings* that build community with and shared commitments to one another and the group
3. *Informal classroom circles* to discuss content and issues that affect the group
4. *Impromptu conferences* to resolve low-level problems that arise in the classroom

More formal practices are reserved for restoring damaged relationships. In these cases, trained facilitators lead groups to resolve high-stakes problems such as verbal and physical confrontations, property damage, use of prohibited substances, and so on. The three more formal practices, which we elaborate on in Chapter 5, are as follows:

1. *Formal classroom circles* to resolve a problem within the group
2. *Victim-offender dialogues* to resolve conflict, allow the victim to address the offender, and allow the offender to show remorse and make amends to the victim
3. *High-stakes conferences* that involve the victim's and the offender's families and other community members to evaluate incidents that might require the involvement of law enforcement

Affective Statements and Questions

The language we use in the classroom can either foster students' social and emotional development or tear it down. We deeply admire the work of Peter Johnston, whose research on the use of language in the classroom has influenced the work we do at our school. Johnston writes about language as *constitutive* and *positional,* meaning that it "creates realities . . . invites identities . . . and position[s] people in relation to one another" (2004, p. 9). In other words, the language we use influences how students see themselves and, in turn, how others view them. It is for this reason that we are wary of discipline strategies that communicate to others some sort of difference in status among students. Whether it's moving clothespins on a chart or using an app to award and deduct points to and from students, these strategies remind them that there's a hierarchy in place and fosters a competitive rather than collaborative climate.

Identity-Building Statements

Students' senses of identity and agency are critical to restorative practices because they influence the extent to which students can solve problems, assume ownership of situations, and take action to make improvements. Identity-building statements allow students to examine themselves and the roles they devise for themselves. When we refer to students according to a certain category of identity (e.g., as English scholars, historians, or expert investigators), the students are challenged to consider the characteristics of that identity and whether or not they apply to them. When we ask students identity-building questions that contain labels ("I wonder if, as a writer, you're ready for this?"), we simultaneously provide them with an identity and challenge them to extend themselves. When students misbehave, teachers can use restorative identity labels to separate the students from their actions: a statement like "That's not the Robert I know" communicates that you see the individual behind the event.

Agency Statements

These types of statements provide students with the confidence to act. Statements such as "I can tell you studied hard for this biology test" and "That hard work is really paying off for you" signal to students that effort bears results. By contrast, statements such as "You're so smart," although well intended, can paralyze learners by implying that intelligence is innate—what Yeager and Dweck (2012) call a fixed mindset. Agency statements are not reserved for positive events. Consider the following: "I can see that you put time into practicing for the tryout, but it didn't work out for you. Why do you think that happened, and what will you do next time?" Here, the adult lets the student know that although effort alone doesn't guarantee the desired results, his or her resiliency will work toward attaining them.

Affective statements and questions using the word "*I*" allow adults to avoid labels that can negatively affect student identity and agency. We know not to say "You're a bad person" to a student, but "You make me so angry when you do that" isn't much better; students can hear the barely veiled shaming. By contrast, a statement such as "I felt angry when you left the classroom without permission because it embarrasses me when you're caught roaming the halls" shifts the focus to the behavior without generalizing it as a permanent character trait. The statement follows a simple formula: "I felt [emotion] when [behavior or event] because [reason for the emotion]." The same formula can be used to address positive situations, too: "I felt so proud of all of you when you left the room in such an orderly way for the fire drill because it showed me that our practice last week was worth it." When teachers make a habit of using statements that follow this formula, they soon hear students using similar language.

The students in Traci Hansen's 3rd grade class regularly use affective statements to solve problems on their own. Ms. Hansen models using the statements until students develop their own habit. For example, when Ben tore up Alex's paper, Alex said, "Hey, don't do that! I mean, it hurt my feelings when you tore that up because I was still working on it." Ben responded, "Sorry. I thought you were done, and I was just having fun ripping it. Want me to get you a new one?" What could have been an altercation between two boys ended very peacefully, with no hard feelings.

Class Meetings

Class meetings are an important feature of schools dedicated to restorative practices because they build the identity and agency of the class as a whole. Typically, such meetings serve one or more of the following purposes: to plan and make decisions, to "check in," and to solve problems or raise awareness (Vance, 2013). Both academic and social issues are appropriate topics for consideration. Class meetings are usually student-led, which helps learners "become motivated and take responsibility for their behavior, their work, and their class participation" (Leachman & Victor, 2003, p. 64). As Potter and Davis (2003) note, research shows that implementing class meetings three times a week for eight weeks "increased students' skills in relation to listening attentively, complimenting and appreciating others, showing respect for others, and building a sense of community" (p. 88).

We don't recommend using class meetings for conflict resolution among students—that's what conferences are for. Instead, we recommend using them as vehicles for discussing matters openly with the whole class. Rules for class meetings ought to ensure that all classroom voices are heard. The teacher's role in these meetings is primarily that of facilitator, posing questions for the class to discuss (e.g., "What is something we should make sure we're all doing tomorrow so that our trip to the museum goes well?"). Older students might hold short discussions about the learning strategies they find most effective in the class. As students become comfortable with class meeting routines, teachers can ask them to take the lead as facilitators.

Elementary teachers routinely have daily class meetings in the morning that usually involve the teacher and students greeting each other, sharing news, and conducting daily routines such as noting the weather or date. Students can use these meetings to recognize peers, raise classroom issues, and ask clarifying questions. Some teachers end each day with a second class meeting to debrief the day's events, discuss students' progress toward daily goals, and preview the next day's lesson. For example, kindergarten teacher Ashlee King uses class meetings to preview the text students will be listening to the following day. "I often provide students with a question or two to ask their families to start discussion at home," she said. "Tomorrow we're going to be reading about the change of seasons, so today I suggested that my students ask family members to identify their favorite season and explain why they like it. These prompts give us all something to talk about the next morning."

Class meetings build connectedness and affiliation within the group, thereby strengthening relationships that might be tested throughout the year. Grant and Davis (2012) offer the example of a 1st grade teacher who began to notice that her students were splitting off into hierarchical groups. To understand the network of relationships among her students, she privately asked each of them to name the three classmates they would like to play with at recess. She then labeled the students whose names most frequently came up as "stars" and the ones who were never named as "isolates." For the next six weeks, she held daily class meetings to discuss topics that the students themselves suggested. When the six weeks were over, the teacher once again surveyed her students about whom they'd most like to play with at recess—and this time, no student counted as either a star or an isolate.

Often, the first thing teachers do when implementing class meetings is to ensure a consistent agenda. For example, middle school science teacher Janis Clark likes to ask her students the following questions at each meeting to focus on solving problems that the class is facing:

- What is the problem our class is having?
- Why is this a problem?
- How does the problem make you feel?
- What can we do about the problem? Let's brainstorm solutions.
- What is our best solution?

High school English teacher Eric Matapang employs the same generic agenda for every meeting:

1. Call to Order
2. Encouragement Circle
3. Old Business
4. New Business
5. Shout-Outs
6. Close Meeting

Mr. Matapang's students engage in class meetings at least twice a week. One of his students, Leandro, explained to us the value that the meetings held for him: "We know that there will always be a time to talk about stuff, so we can focus on the class at the other times. Like, once, I really didn't understand a big project, but I didn't stress because I knew that we had a meeting the next day and I could ask then. It's just good to have time to talk as a group."

"It kinda feels like we've grown up," added Leandro's classmate Marisol. "We have to handle things on our own, we have to make decisions, and we have to respect each other so that we can all be heard and make good decisions."

During the Encouragement Circle portion of the meetings, each student turns to the person on his or her left and offers an encouraging statement related to the other's success, thus helping to build a growth mindset (Dweck, 2006). For example, one student might say to another, "I saw you helping the new kid with annotations in physics class. That made me want to be a better person, too."

The Old Business portion of Mr. Matapang's meetings is kept brief. Discussions during the New Business portion are based on written suggestions that students add to a box on the corner of Mr. Matapang's desk. Topic suggestions range from seating arrangements to stressful assignments to plans for field studies. Sometimes students will suggest discussing major events in the community, as was recently the case when a student from a neighboring school was killed while street racing.

If there is time, the meeting continues with the Shout-Outs portion, during which students publicly thank, recognize, or compliment others. One example from Mr. Matapang's class is when Kareem said to Marcello, "I was having a hard time with my mom dying, and I really want to thank you for having my back. I owe you big time. I will never forget." We find this to be an especially powerful part of class meetings once students become comfortable with complimenting one another, as it builds community and allegiance to one another and the school. When students recognize each other, they like school better and tend to behave in ways that are respectful toward the community, resulting in safe, productive learning (Landau & Gathercoal, 2000).

Sometimes teachers worry that they won't be able to cover all of their lessons if they devote time to class meetings and other informal restorative practices activities. Our experience suggests that class meetings ensure that learning is really happening throughout the day. Informal processes allow students' worries and fears to be addressed so that they can focus on the lessons during instructional time. An investment in class meetings can result in a peaceful classroom climate where learning, both social and academic, flourishes.

Informal Classroom Circles

The use of circles to facilitate discussion is arguably the most distinctive element of restorative practices. Unlike class meetings, during

setting up the space

which students might sit on a rug or at their desks, circles consist of chairs arranged facing inward, without desks or tables to serve as visual or psychological barriers. This physical arrangement primes students to expect a high level of interaction, including listening. Off-task behaviors decrease significantly in circle arrangements, perhaps due to students' senses of increased accountability to the group (Rosenfield, Lambert, & Black, 1985). Informal circles are intended to allow students to answer truthfully and honestly to questions or prompts.

For resolving conflicts, we encourage the use of formal circles (discussed further in Chapter 5). We learned this lesson during the first year that we adopted restorative practices: without intending to, the only times we used circles were to resolve conflicts—and within a month, students equated "circling up" (dragging their chairs to the center of the room) with disciplinary action of some sort. Dominique soon discovered that the moment he walked into a classroom to facilitate a circle, students would ask one another, "Who did something wrong?" In due course, we came to understand that students need informal circles to discuss issues unrelated to conflicts.

need both informal & formal

One well-known version of the informal circles strategy is the Socratic seminar, in which participants delve into a topic, text, or issue of study. For example, a high school English class might employ a Socratic seminar to discuss the trial and death of Tom Robinson and the relative culpability of other characters in *To Kill a Mockingbird* (Lee, 1960/2002). Similarly, a 4th grade classroom might use a Socratic seminar to examine the development of Bud's personal rules about lying in *Bud, Not Buddy* (Curtis, 2004). Types of informal circles include sequential and nonsequential circles, fishbowls, and inside-outside circles (Costello et al., 2010). ✗

multiple types

Sequential Circles

Sequential circles have a fixed order for member participation, and each student is encouraged to participate. This type of circle can help

[Handwritten margin notes: "each kid shares, can opt out, helpful for quick check ins" and "academic" / "social"]

students who might otherwise sit quietly and observe. The teacher serves as facilitator, posing a question for the group to consider. A talking piece—that is, an item that serves as a visual reminder of who is speaking—is passed around the circle, and students take turns offering a brief response to the question. Importantly, students who aren't holding the talking piece do not respond directly to those who are, though they may refer to their comments when it's their turn to speak. Students always have the option to forfeit their turns, although we have found that they do so less often as they become more comfortable with the process. Teachers can use sequential circles to check in with students at the beginning of a lesson or to "check out" at the end.

High school world history teacher Joanna Schaefer uses sequential circles to debrief lessons with students. For example, after conducting a close reading of a speech by Joseph Stalin, Ms. Schaefer convened a circle for students to share their impressions. Students used words such as *intimidating* and *frightening* to describe the Soviet dictator and his words. A week later, Ms. Schaefer reconvened the circle for students to discuss Franklin Roosevelt's "Day of Infamy" speech; this time, students described the speaker as "calming," "assuring," and "determined."

Informal sequential circles are also helpful for broaching especially sensitive topics. For example, high school English teacher Heather Anderson convened a circle with her students to discuss their feelings about an upcoming high-stakes exit exam. Anxieties were running high, and Ms. Anderson asked each student to describe how he or she felt at that moment. "They had a chance to hear that they weren't alone in feeling nervous," she said. "Too many times, kids this age think they're the only one experiencing something."

Nonsequential Circles

Unlike sequential circles, nonsequential circles do not have a fixed order and allow students to respond directly to one another as frequently as they care to. Thus, students who are truly engaged in the topic have more time to speak in depth about it.

Eighth grade health teacher Julia Stephens-Martin held a non-sequential circle to discuss an upcoming school board decision regarding the sale of snacks and drinks at fund-raisers. Some students argued that snack and drink sales were necessary to support extracurricular activities and clubs; others argued that the school shouldn't sanction the sale of items that don't meet the district's nutrition requirements. "I'm not sure they came to any consensus through this circle," said Ms. Stephens-Martin, "but I was really pleased with how they listened respectfully to opposing views. I wish all meetings were conducted so civilly."

Fishbowls

These types of circles are particularly effective for skill building and for discussing sensitive topics that require careful listening. The fishbowl strategy uses two circles, one small inner circle surrounded by a larger observing circle. Students in the inner circle discuss a topic, while those in the outside circle observe and take notes. In some cases, membership in the inner and outer circles remains constant throughout the duration of the circle; in other cases, students are invited to exit the inner circle when they have finished talking, leaving an open chair for a member of the outer circle to take.

At the beginning of the school year, 6th grade science teacher Rosa Vasquez invited six students from the year before to model the use of fishbowl circles for her current students. The inner circle of 7th graders discussed the merits of recycling and whether or not homeowners should be fined for not doing it, and the observing circle of 6th graders took notes. Over time, and with practice, the students in Ms. Vasquez's class learned how to engage in this type of interaction and used it for a variety of academic and nonacademic conversations.

modeling a convo; inviting new voices [handwritten margin note]

[handwritten in margin: rotating conversation partners]

Inside-Outside Circles

At our school, we refer to these as "speed dating" circles. Like fishbowls, inside-outside circles include a small circle encircled by a larger one, but in this case students in the inner circle face out and partner with a student from the larger circle. At the teacher's prompt, the partners talk about a topic for a few minutes. Then, at another prompt, students in the inner circle rotate clockwise, so that all eventually work together.

Ninth grade teacher Sarah Soriano coordinates inside-outside circles that include her students and 11th and 12th grade members of a mentorship program known as the Connect Crew. Mentors occupy the inner circle and spend a few minutes engaged in social conversation with each 9th grader in the outer circle. After the freshmen have met all the mentors, they complete an online survey listing the three mentors they'd prefer to have. Each of the Connect Crew mentors then receives a caseload of 9th graders to check in with regularly. According to Ms. Soriano, the mentors serve as effective advocates for students with whom teachers can consult.

Kindergarten teacher David Leong uses inside-outside circles during mathematics instruction. "Number sense is huge in kindergarten, as is completing one-digit addition under 10," he said. "All the students have a few counting cubes in their hands and a pencil and paper. Each set of partners has to figure out how many cubes they have in total and then write it as an equation."

"They're not used to completing tasks this quickly," he added, "but the inside-outside circles help them to increase their fluency in counting and addition."

Tips for Running Informal Circles

Teachers need to communicate their expectations about the use of circles clearly to all students and go over them every time circles are employed. For informal circles to be effective, students must know that they are in a safe environment and have the ability to speak freely. For this reason, we would suggest including an expectation for students to listen as allies even when they are not in agreement.

Circles help students build and sustain trust with one another to solve problems together as a community. However, the community is diminished if a few students dominate the discussion. Circles should provide all students with an opportunity to speak if they want. It is critical to let students know that all voices are needed. Some teachers encourage students to respond to comments without feeling rushed but also concisely and respectfully of others.

Circles offer teachers a way to check in with students and assess their learning by listening closely to them. They should observe the conversations among students and use them as a basis for future lesson plans. For example, 5th grade teacher Yolanda Baker met with her students in an informal circle to find out how they were progressing toward completion of their first research project of the year.

"You have the science research report due in one week," she said to her students. "I'd like to know what you're struggling with."

As the talking piece went around the circle, Ms. Baker took notes about her students' responses but kept silent. When the students had all had a chance to share, she asked them to form groups based on shared concerns regarding the project.

"As you meet in your groups, see if you can build a team to support one another," she said. "We'll devote tomorrow morning to doing some troubleshooting together, and I'll meet with each of the teams."

Later that same day, Ms. Baker explained her approach to us. "I could sense there was a lot of general anxiety, but rather than reteach everything, it made a lot more sense to target support where it's needed. I'm looking forward to tomorrow, and I hope they feel more confident by the end of the day."

Teachers should be sure not to rush the circles, as students may be more reluctant to speak than they might seem. This was the case when 6th grade teacher Kevin Naderhoff convened a circle and asked his students to name a challenge they were facing and a triumph they had enjoyed. It was the second day of school, and the students' reluctance to speak really showed in the circle. Mr. Naderhoff realized that most of the students didn't know one another and were hesitant to reveal themselves.

Suspecting that he had pressed his students to speak more freely than they were prepared to, Mr. Naderhoff said, "I think I asked too much of you just now. Let's try this in a different way. Go back to your desks and interview the person sitting next to you. You'll then introduce that person to the rest of us."

For the next 10 minutes, students learned a bit about one another and took notes. When Mr. Naderhoff reconvened the circle, they were ready to talk. "They needed more time to prepare, and talking with one other person made identifying a challenge and a triumph easier," he said. "I need to remember that growing this community means that I have to nurture it."

Impromptu Conferences

Conflicts usually occur when a combination of anxiety, frustration, and fear boils over (Morris, 1998). It follows, then, that teachers can reduce conflict by creating conditions that prevent such feelings from occurring. However, anxiety, frustration, and fear can never be completely eliminated, so students need tools for resolving minor conflicts before they erupt into major incidences. Working as facilitators, teachers can convene impromptu conferences to help students resolve situations that threaten their relationships and disrupt their learning.

When teachers see conflict brewing, they should resist the temptation to simply issue a command ("Knock it off now"), because the command doesn't teach the students anything. Instead, we suggest promoting communication between the two parties. Here's an example:

Teacher: I just saw the two of you pushing one another out of the line. I got worried that you could hurt one another. What's happening?

Student 1: I was here first, and he cut in front of me.

Teacher: [To student 2] How would you describe the situation?

Student 2: I was here before him, but then I was talking to Justin and I lost my place. He took it.

Teacher: It makes me kind of afraid when I see students pushing each other in the cafeteria line. How does it make each of you feel when you see that happening with other students?

Student 2: Like I have to fight to get into the line.

Student 1: The same. And like I won't get a turn.

Teacher: I agree. I think it makes the little ones believe that they have to fight to get into line. That's not something I want them to believe. I know you have younger brothers and sisters at this school. What do you want them to learn?

Student 1: That they don't have to fight, 'cause the cafeteria's not gonna run out of food.

Student 2: [giggling] Unless it's bean-and-cheese burrito day!

Teacher: It seems like the two of you agree on lots of things. Can you solve this?

Student 1: Go ahead and go in front of me. It's teriyaki beef dippers today.

Impromptu conferences are one way to resolve conflicts quickly before they get any bigger. Along the way, students develop skills to solve minor conflicts on their own. The example above includes many of the elements that are essential to successful impromptu conferences:

(handwritten margin note: Key elements ① Impromptu conferences ★)

- It's brief.
- Students aren't threatened with punishment.
- The teacher asked each student for his version of what happened.
- The teacher shared her own feelings.
- The teacher reminded the students that they are accountable to others.
- The teacher asked the students to suggest ways to resolve the problem.
- The teacher modeled how to communicate with someone who disagrees with you.

Of course, students will sometimes have conflicts that teachers don't initially see and that students ask them to solve. Rather than impose a judgment, it's wise for teachers to give students a chance to resolve their issues with your help.

When Nancy taught 4th grade, she set up a "peace table" in her classroom for resolving student conflicts. It really wasn't much—just a desk with a feathered pen in a holder. Whenever students had a conflict, they were each to draft a "peace-table statement" before coming together to meet with Nancy. Every statement had to have three distinct elements:

1. An explanation of what the disagreement was about.
2. An "I" statement explaining the writer's feelings ("When you _____, I felt _____. I would like _____.").
3. An "I" statement explaining what the writer thinks the other person might say ("When you _____, I felt _____. I would like _____.").

Next, Nancy would meet with both students to discuss the conflict. She found that the time the students spent drafting accomplished two important objectives: it gave both parties time to cool off, and it encouraged both to put the conflict in perspective. In most cases, the conflict was on its way to being resolved before the impromptu conference even took place. Nancy knew that her students were progressing when she overheard two boys squabbling on their way back from recess, only to hear one comment, "We better figure this out, or we'll have to go to the peace table again!"

Writing can be of benefit for students whose emotions are running high. The process provides them with a cooling-off period during which they can gather their thoughts. Some teachers we know have transformed Jack Canfield's (1986) Total Truth Process into a series of sentence starters to help students in conflict prepare for conversations. This process allows students to begin by expressing their anger and then progress through a series of emotions leading up to compassion and forgiveness. As Canfield notes, "The reason I call it the total truth is that often, when we're upset, we fail to communicate all our true feelings to the person we're upset with. We get stuck at the level of anger or pain and rarely move past it to emotional completion. As a result, it can be difficult to feel close to—or even at ease with—the other person after such an angry or painful confrontation" (p. 225). For the process to be effective, Canfield suggests that students should spend time expressing their feelings in each of the stages. Here are some possible sentence starters for each:

moving from anger to forgiveness

1. **Anger and resentment**—I'm angry that . . . , I hate that . . . , I'm fed up with . . . , I resent . . .
2. **Hurt**—It hurt me when . . . , I felt sad when . . . , I feel hurt that . . . , I feel disappointed about . . .
3. **Fear**—I was afraid that . . . , I feel scared when . . . , I get afraid of you when . . . , I'm afraid that I . . .

4. **Remorse, regret, and accountability**—I'm sorry that . . . , Please forgive me for . . . , I'm sorry for . . . , I didn't mean to . . .

5. **Want**—All I ever wanted was . . . , I want you to . . . , I wanted . . . , I deserve . . .

6. **Love, compassion, forgiveness, and appreciation**—I understand that . . . , I appreciate . . . , I love you for . . . , I forgive you for . . . , Thank you for . . .

Teacher Don Bragg used these sentence starters to prepare two 7th grade girls for a discussion about a dispute about a group work assignment. He placed the two students in different corners of the classroom and had them articulate their feelings in writing. Here's what Melody wrote:

> I'm angry that you didn't finish the part of the group presentation you said you'd have done today. I was hurt because you didn't act like you even cared, because you just laughed it off. I'm afraid that I am going to get a bad grade because you didn't do your part of the work. I didn't mean to insult you by calling you a bitch. I just want you to keep your promises. I understand that you're my friend, but when you don't keep your word it makes it hard to be your friend.

And here's Vanessa's statement:

> I'm angry that you swore at me and called me a bad word. I was hurt because we promised that we would never disrespect each other this way. I'm afraid that you are fed up with me and will stop being friends. I didn't mean to let you down with the project. I forgot it was due today. I want you to tell me when you're mad but not get so nasty. That's not what BFFs do. I understand that I put you in a bad place and I'm sorry.

Students are often not aware of their insights in advance of writing. It is a process, with sentence stems leading them on a path toward ownership of the situation. It took Melody and Vanessa a good 15 minutes to finish half a dozen sentences. After reading the two statements himself, Mr. Bragg asked the girls to silently read each other's papers. It's probably not a surprise to learn the two were in tears a few minutes later and ended up hugging. By addressing their heightened feelings first, Mr. Bragg was able to help the girls move forward to discuss the status of their group project.

Conflicts such as Melody and Vanessa's are best addressed in the classroom, under the guidance of a caring adult who is willing to spend the time helping the students untangle their conflicts. As Mr. Bragg later remarked to us, "Yeah, I teach science, but I teach middle school kids. Science is my content—kids are why I'm here."

Impromptu conferences are not limited to minor conflicts between students; teachers can also use them to address conflicts that they themselves may be having with students. Most often, such conferences center on addressing students' off-task behavior.

All of us, students and adults alike, go off-task at some point. Remembering this can help us to restrain our emotions when it happens.

Math teacher Craig Kenny noticed a group of students who seemed to be off-task in his 9th grade class one day, so he posted a problem on the board for the rest of the class to solve while he met with them. "I'm not sure what happened, but it seemed like you were not paying attention to the lesson," he said. "I was disappointed because I worked really hard to plan this lesson that I thought you would really enjoy and that would teach you how to figure out problems with exponents. Is there something that I should know?"

"I'm sorry, it was my fault," said one of the students. "Coach told me that our game was changed to a different place, and I was letting the other guys know. Then we started talking about the other team, and we got out of control. We're back on our game now. We didn't mean to disrespect you, but we did."

Mr. Kenny accepted the apology. Then, pointing to the board, he said, "Can you work that problem and call me over if you need some help? I really want to make sure that you got this process down."

This brief interaction resulted in the students returning to their work and attempting to repair the harm they had caused. Scolding them in front of the class or sending them to the vice principal would have taken much longer, resulted in hurt feelings, and prevented a lot of learning.

Teachers can also use impromptu conferences to discuss academic issues with students. For example, 7th grade teacher Laura Kearns held an impromptu conference with a student, Cynthia, who did poorly on a recent test. "You didn't do very well on the science test, right?" she asked the student. "My goal is for you to learn this information. I really think it's important, because you might be the one who figures out the next recycling program or how to reduce the garbage patch in the Pacific Ocean. Can you tell me what happened?"

"I just gave up," said Cynthia. "I got confused on some of the words, so I just quit. I didn't really think it was that important. I didn't know you cared so much about this. Or me."

"I do care about you," said Ms. Kearns. "A lot! I care about you more than the science, and I love science. I want you to love science as much as I do. Do you want to review this with me this afternoon and then try the test again? I think you know the information because I've seen you work in a group. You never give up, and you help your classmates. It's really impressive."

Cynthia smiled. "Wow," she said. "I knew coming to this school was different, but I never thought I'd have a teacher meet with me like this. Yes, I'll try again. Thank you."

Students should do a lot of the talking during conferences. To ensure that students participate in the conversation, we have developed a series of questions that teachers can use (see Figure 4.1). The questions vary based on the situation. (It's important to remember

4.1 Sample Questions and Statements for Impromptu Conferences

For conferences with individual students who are struggling behaviorally or academically:

1. How do you describe yourself?

2. How do other people describe you?

3. What assumptions do teachers make about you that are not true?

4. How would you like others to describe you?

5. Let's make a plan to get you where you want to be.

For conferences with individual students who are doing well:

1. How do you describe yourself?

2. What assumptions do teachers make about you that are not true?

3. What are we doing that is helping you reach your goals?

4. What should we be doing more or less of to help you reach your goals?

5. Let's make a plan to get you where you want to be.

For discussing *what* students want to be:

1. What do you like to do, and can that be a career?

2. How do people who do that for a living prepare for this career?

3. Let's find out what you need to do in middle school/high school to put you on that path.

4. Are you on track to reach this goal?

5. Let's make a plan to reach your goals.

For discussing *who* students want to be:

1. When do you feel proud of yourself, inside or outside of school?

2. Why did you feel that way?

3. What obstacles did you overcome, and how did you do it?

4. What obstacle is holding you back right now?

5. Could some of those same strategies you used to overcome obstacles be used in this situation?

6. Let's make a plan to overcome that obstacle. I bet you're already feeling proud of yourself for tackling this.

that impromptu conferences are not reserved for addressing problematic behavior. They can also be used when things are going really well or to help a student develop some attributes.)

Student Voices: "I Used to Get Laughed At"

Miriam is, admittedly, a bit awkward. She's bigger than most of her 4th grade peers and outspoken about her beliefs and expectations. She often misses social cues and intrudes into conversations, sometimes abruptly leaving others behind. Her teacher, Samantha Lynn, uses class meetings and circles on a regular basis, during which Miriam often expresses her concerns about the way her classmates treat her.

A few weeks into the school year, Miriam was complaining less and complimenting her classmates more. In a class meeting after about eight weeks, Miriam said, "Fernando told me that I was his friend. He is my first friend in 4th grade." Over the course of the year, Miriam developed more friendships. She continued to complain about things, but less about the way people treated her personally and more about bullying that she observed among others. The class came together to address the issues she raised and agreed on solutions, such as launching a peer-led antibullying campaign (with the principal's permission) and creating a public service announcement in iMovie that included the phrase "Sticks and stones can break my bones, but words can hurt forever."

During a circle in late winter, Miriam choked up well before it was her turn to speak. When the talking object—a photo of the class visiting a local organic farm—came to her, Miriam spoke.

"I used to get laughed at," she said. "I got teased and even pushed. People said I was fat. That I was ugly. And stupid. I hated going to school. Now I love it, because of all of the people in this picture. I'm sorry that I wasn't very nice when I first came to this school. But I'm happy that I did. My mom says that I even like myself now."

5 | Peacemaking: Strategic Implementation of Formal Restorative Practices

We have all been wronged. Sometimes these wrongs are fairly minor in the big scheme of things; other times they are significant and painful. We do not want to discount the harm that students, staff, teachers, administrators, and parents can cause to others, as it can be very damaging to relationships and thus compromise students' ability to learn and teachers' ability to teach. When wrongs occur, we demand justice—but it's how we define *justice* that matters.

As we've noted, traditional discipline efforts focus on determining guilt and punishing the offender. In this context, justice means that the offender receives an undesirable consequence that typically involves shame, isolation, and exclusion. Restorative practices take a more educative approach, mobilizing resources to ensure that students continue to learn. *does our approach to justice allow for learning?*

Think about a time when you were personally wronged, intentionally or unintentionally. We were challenged with this prompt during our first professional development session focused on restorative practices. Teachers, staff members, and leaders were asked to write a journal entry about a specific experience, knowing that they would be asked to share their experience with a peer.

The issues we discussed were humbling and sad. Our colleagues experienced some pretty awful things. One colleague spoke about being violated by someone she thought was a friend who broke into her Facebook account, posted several inappropriate comments, and sent messages that were "just plain wrong" to friends. Another colleague shared the emotional harm she had endured from a former spouse. Someone else talked about a former boss who belittled people when they made mistakes. Another talked about being bullied in middle school. All of the incidents discussed had occurred over seven years ago—in one case, 33 years ago. Clearly, none of us had resolved our issues completely, even though "justice" of some sort had been served in many cases (the abusive spouse spent time in rehab, the belittling boss was terminated for misconduct, the middle school bully was suspended). After all these years, one of our colleagues continued to ask, "What was it about me that let that person think he could harm me?" Another still wondered, "Why was I the target? What did I do? I still wish I could find out."

Next, the facilitator asked us to ask each other the following questions:

- How did you feel?
- What questions did you want to ask the offender?
- What else did you want to say to him or her?
- Who or what could make things right for you?
- What would justice have looked like for you?

The ensuing conversations further confirmed the long-term effects of unresolved conflicts. We had to ask ourselves if we wanted our students to suffer the same fates. Our students may not go through experiences as difficult as those of our colleagues, but we still want them to attain closure following a conflict. As one of our colleagues put it, "I really just wanted an apology and maybe a commitment that it wouldn't happen again."

Our next task was to consider a time when we'd caused another person harm, either intentionally or unintentionally. We were told that we did not have to share this experience with anyone else but that we should write some notes to ourselves as we recalled it. As part of the reflection, we were asked to consider the following questions:

(margin annotation: 2-way conversation)

- How did you feel?
- What would you have liked to say to the victim?
- Who or what would have made things right?
- What would justice have looked like for you and for the victim?

We spent about 10 minutes in quiet, personal reflection. When we came back together as a group, we were asked how we answered the questions. As our facilitator explained, "I would like us to talk about what would have made things right. What would justice look like to you now, with some distance from the event?"

Again, the conversation was powerful. The most common theme was a strong desire to apologize, to make things right, and to let the victim know why we had done what we'd done. As one of our colleagues said, "I wish I could do it over. I want to apologize. I want to own it. I was wrong, really wrong. I just want to tell her why it happened and beg for forgiveness." Another said, "I wish I could tell him that I suffered as well. I beat myself up over it, and I want to apologize. Really, I'd do whatever it took to make things right."

Overcoming Resistance

The reason we spent so much time focused on the subject of justice during the professional development session discussed above is that the adults in a school have to be comfortable and supportive of restorative practices if they are going to be effective. A permanent change in students' behavior may not occur after a single restorative conference—but permanent change doesn't occur after suspension or expulsion, either. We have found that educators need to clarify their thinking about justice if restorative practices are to truly take hold, which requires a significant shift in thinking—as Zehr (2002) notes, the restorative practices approach is a philosophy rather than a method.

For restorative practices to work, we have to learn to separate the deed from the doer (Braithwaite, 1989). Students need to know that they are valued but that the behavior is unacceptable. Australian criminologist John Braithwaite (1989) has found that people who are shamed and stigmatized for their actions are far more likely to reoffend than those who aren't. But addressing conflicts or misbehavior in a nonstigmatizing way is easier said than done. We tend to conflate people's actions with their fundamental selves, and we often criticize both. If we are to restore classrooms and schools to healthy learning communities, we have to focus on the actions without rejecting the individuals. When teachers say to elementary school students "Don't be a bad boy" or "Do you always have to do that?" they run the risk of leaving students with a sense that they, rather than their actions, are the problem.

We are reminded of a middle school student who said very mean things to teachers, often targeting physical characteristics that the adults were self-conscious about. One of the student's teachers said to him, "You are such an interesting thinker, and your art is fantastic. I'm just surprised you talk that way to people. Do you know that you can hurt people's feelings with words?" By contrast, another of his teachers said to him, "You should be ashamed of yourself. You have no respect for adults. If I had my way, you'd be suspended every day until you were out of here." Any guess as to which teacher had a better year? Jacob's behavior was totally different in each teacher's classroom, largely because one of his teachers was able to separate the deed from the doer and work to change the deed. The other teacher made it clear that Jacob should be excluded and would never feel welcomed.

[handwritten margin note: maintain hope in human dignity even while addressing the situation]

We have to learn to focus on restitution rather than consequences. We have to remember that punishments only work when students get caught. In such cases, they'll focus on what to do next time to avoid detection rather than reflect and learn from the experience. Students will alter their behavior to avoid being punished, not because they have developed an internal locus of control or a moral compass.

Brandi, a 3rd grader, often steals things from the desks of other students. Her teacher and then her principal have used a progressive discipline policy with her, escalating consequences with every offense: a scolding the first time, then sending her to the office, and, finally, suspending her.

At the suspension meeting, Brandi's mother was shocked by her daughter's behavior. "Why are you stealing things?" she asked. "You have all of those things! Kids in your class don't like you because you're a thief. And they're going to tease you. I didn't raise a thief. I'm so angry at you! You little *thief*."

Observing the mother's outburst, the principal realized that his disciplinary approach wasn't working.

"I think we need some time to create a new plan," said the principal to Brandi's mom. "We've been focused on trying to get Brandi's behavior to stop by applying consequences. Maybe we need to try something else. Maybe you could take Brandi home today and talk more about why she is compelled to take things. I don't think you raised a thief, but I do think we need to get to the bottom of why Brandi is doing this."

As we have noted before, we're not totally opposed to suspension in specific cases. We just don't see it as a learning opportunity for students. We know that suspensions can provide some time for staff to develop a plan and for students to cool off a bit. That's why it makes sense in Brandi's case: she, her teacher, and the principal all needed some time to think about what to do next. Just as the educators had focused on applying consequences, Brandi had focused on getting better at taking objects that didn't belong to her. Her teacher and principal hadn't thought to ask what motivated her behavior or how she might restore the harm that she'd caused with her actions.

The plan Brandi's teacher and principal eventually developed focused on having her face her victims and also meet with a social worker (pending her mother's approval) to identify her motivations. Though such a plan may seem obvious in retrospect, it's easy to think that a little punishment or a few consequences will solve a problem when you're in the thick of it.

When Brandi met with the social worker, she told her that she didn't understand why she wanted to take things from other students. She also talked about her parents' separation and not getting much attention from her father of late. When the social worker analyzed Brandi's behavior further, she noticed that Brandi consistently stole from boys' desks and that when the boys found out they would often yell at her.

The new plan to address Brandi's behavior included having her face her victims so she could learn how they felt when they realized she'd taken something of theirs. The plan also included set-aside time for Brandi to interact with others in a positive way, such as by reading aloud to kindergartners after finishing her tasks, as well as ongoing counseling with the social worker and her family.

Making Peace

When implementing restorative practices, we should learn to ask, "How will the student restore damaged relationships?" rather than,

"What are the consequences for the student's actions?" Restorative plans should ask offending students to

- Acknowledge their behavior.
- Apologize.
- Express repentance.
- Commit not to repeat the offense.
- Offer to make amends.

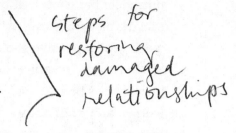

Steps for restoring damaged relationships

These requirements are a far cry from the types of consequences normally found in schools. They have the potential to permanently change students' future behaviors by developing their internal control mechanisms and empathy toward others (Curwin & Mendler, 1997).

Restorative practices must be about reintegration, not marginalization. Offending students need to return to their regular environment as soon as possible so that relationships can be repaired and academic learning can continue. As Braithwaite (1989) notes, offenders who cannot restore the relationships they've damaged will often develop new relationships with fellow offenders who are similarly alienated. These new relationships can devolve into a subculture of wrongdoers who see no need to comply with the rules, much less develop positive habits and relationships with people who do.

We are reminded of Cody, an 11th grader who had been caught smoking marijuana at lunch—it was his first time trying the drug. In many schools, Cody would have been suspended and marginalized, which runs the risk of shifting Cody's allegiance from adults and positive peer role models to students who will lead him further astray. But having a conversation with a student who is under the influence of drugs wouldn't be productive either, so the school called his parents, informed them of the situation, and asked them to pick him up and supervise him for the rest of the day. A meeting was scheduled for the following day to let Cody know that his choice to use drugs was not

OK, because he was a valuable member of the learning community. The principal met with Cody's mom when she arrived to pick him up and let her know that they were not considering suspension and that the meeting they'd scheduled was intended to recruit Cody into making more positive choices.

During the meeting the following day, Cody heard how he had hurt various people. He faced his coach, a favorite teacher, a social worker, and, with Cody's mom's permission, a student leader who had been trained in restorative practices. The meeting focused on respect for the school and the people in it, the importance of not creating hazards, and Cody's role as a leader in the school. His mom expressed her hurt, worry, and fears. She also said that she planned to drug test him monthly. "Not because I don't trust you, honey— I do," she told him. "I just need the peace of mind. I hope you'll understand."

Cody admitted his transgression, apologized for the harm he had caused, and made a commitment to stay clean. He also told his mom that she could drug test him. "I know that you want the best for me, even when I get angry at you," he said. "You've handled this great, and I'm sorry that you had to deal with this." He then asked if he could join an after-school club "because I get in trouble when I have too much free time."

"I think we should touch base at least twice per week for the next couple of weeks," added the social worker, "just to see that you're on track. Then we can drop it to once a week, and if all is going well, you can just come to see me when you want."

In Cody's case, the elapsed time between his offense and his reintegration into the learning environment was quite short. Some might say that he should have been suspended or even expelled. But a restorative approach acknowledges that young people make mistakes in the process of growing up and that these mistakes provide them with an opportunity to learn.

Types of Formal Restorative Practices

Formal restorative practices are used to address significant problems that are unlikely to be resolved without an investment in time and dialogue. Mullet (2014) argues that conversations in such situations must be respectful and allow all perspectives to be heard before any further action is taken. She suggests that educators follow a three-phase process to help students repair relationships, address the harm they've done, and support each other as they internalize the process and develop positive habits of their own. The process works as follows:

Phase 1: Unwind. In the first phase, those who have been harmed have an opportunity to voice their feelings in private. They are encouraged to calm down—to unwind, if you will—from the hurt they've experienced. Because conflict can damage a person's sense of self, part of the Unwind conversation focuses on reestablishing the offended party's identity. Another part of the conversation focuses on soliciting ideas from the victim regarding ways to allow for restitution, repair, and healing.

processing first w/ those who are harmed

Phase 2: Rewind. During this phase, the offending student is given the opportunity to reflect on his or her behavior and understand the harm that it caused. This phase allows students to review the situation, consider the facts, and identify a course of action to make things right. The goal of the Rewind phase is to induce empathy in students and ensure that they accept responsibility for their actions. Students can practice their apologies during this phase and identify what they consider to be reasonable consequences for their behavior.

then w/ offender for empathy & understanding

Phase 3: Windup. During this phase, observers of the conflict have an opportunity to share their perspectives and become participants in the healing process, supporting both the offended and offending parties. Such participation is empowering for students and increases the likelihood that relationships will be repaired and positive behavior continued. Adult observers can take part in the Windup phase as well. Figure 5.1 also contains sample questions useful in the Windup conversation.

From Getting Even to Getting Well

Mullet's three phases for addressing serious conflict can be implemented using a variety of formal restorative processes. As Pranis (2003) notes, formal restorative practices define justice as *getting well* rather than *getting even*. When offending students understand the harm they've caused, they do less of it (Strang & Braithwaite, 2001). We have seen this happen time and again.

Formal processes take time to implement. Listening to students—to those who have been harmed and to those who cause harm—can consume hours of the school day. As Mullet notes, "Restorative-minded educators view getting well as an academic priority and make time during the day for restorative dialogue" (2014, p. 161). As students learn to take care of each other, formal restorative techniques become less frequent. We recommend implementing the following three formal restorative practices in particular:

1. **Formal classroom circles** for resolving conflicts within the class
2. **Victim-offender dialogue** for resolving conflicts, allowing victims to face offenders, and allowing offenders to show remorse and make amends
3. **High-stakes conferences** for addressing serious conflicts that involve larger groups, such as the victim's and the offender's families, and that may require law enforcement involvement

Formal Classroom Circles

Formal classroom circles are appropriate for the Windup phase of Mullet's three-step process for addressing issues that affect the entire learning community, from playground confrontations to student cheating schemes. Because these kinds of incidents can provoke

5.1	Generic Questions Useful in Restorative Conversations

Phase 1: Unwind	• "What happened?" • "Are you alright?" • "How are you feeling now?" • "What do you need now?"/"What will make it better?" • "How can I help?" • "Thanks for . . ."/"I noticed that . . ." (acknowledge the special skills that the student evidences in the conversation or in daily life)
Phase 2: Rewind	• "What happened?" • "What led up to this?" • "What were you thinking at the time?" • "Whom did this affect and how?" • "What do you think about it now?" • "What do you need to do to make it right?" • "How can we make sure this doesn't happen again?" • "Thanks for . . ."/"I noticed that . . ." (affirm a special gift that the student exemplifies to motivate a positive identity)
Phase 3: Windup	• "How did you feel when that happened?" • "What do you need to see happen now?" • "What can you do in such situations?" • "Thanks for . . ."/"I noticed that . . ." (affirm the student's special gift and commitment to preventing future harm)

Source: Mullet, J. H. (2014). Restorative discipline: From getting even to getting well. *Children and Schools, 36*(3), 157–162. Used with permission.

strong reactions among students and teachers alike, formal classroom circles should be run by trained facilitators rather than by the teachers of the students involved. In fact, it might be the teacher rather than the students who needs time to unwind before moving forward. When trained facilitators lead formal classroom circles, teachers are free to express their feelings and listen carefully to their students. If teachers lead the circles on their own, students might see the process as self-serving, and any resulting decisions might lack student buy-in. It's easy for teachers to gather all their students in a circle and lecture them about their behavior for 15 minutes, but it may not be helpful—some students will likely tune out, and others will think they're being blamed for something they didn't do. Most important, this kind of approach fails to shift students from thinking of their own interests to considering the welfare of the group. We want students to see teachers as members of the learning community, and scolding only reinforces an us-versus-them mindset. Meaningful discussion, by contrast, builds a community mindset.

Every classroom should have a talking piece for regulating the flow of the discussion as well as norms regarding its use. Following are the four norms we use for employing the talking piece in a formal circle:

1. "One voice"—a reminder that one person is to speak at a time
2. "Listen with mind and heart"—a reminder to actively consider what others have to say
3. "Safe space"—a reminder to maintain confidentiality
4. "Make space"—a reminder not to dominate the discussion or crowd out the voices of others

It's a good idea for norms to be posted somewhere for the facilitator to use in opening the circle or in case the discussion breaks down.

A few years ago, a teacher's cell phone was stolen from her class during third period. Upset, she decided to meet with Dominique to share her emotions and ask him to facilitate a formal circle with her third-period class the next day. Dominique suggested that they convene a circle in all of her classes so that all her students could discuss the situation, and the teacher agreed.

The next day, Dominique and the teacher convened circles in each of the teacher's classes. Dominique began each circle summarizing what happened and sharing the three questions that would frame the three-round discussion:

1. How does it feel when someone takes something from you?
2. What does a safe classroom feel like?
3. What would you do if you knew that someone had stolen something?

Next, Dominique reminded the class of the norms for the circle and passed the talking piece to the student sitting next to him. When it was the teacher's turn to speak, she was able to express her feelings, crying as she explained that she was upset because the cell phone contained pictures of her recently deceased mother.

After school that day, a student from the teacher's fourth-period class approached Dominique.

"I know who took the phone," he said. "I don't want somebody to have to go through that much pain again."

It's important to understand that the main goal of the circles was not to find out who took the cell phone but, rather, to let the teacher and others express their thoughts about the incident and its detrimental effect on trust in the classroom. By not restricting the circles to the period when the incident happened, Dominique and the teacher were able to show students how many people were affected by it—and in the process they discovered the culprit, who was then the focus of additional restorative activities. Thankfully, the phone was at his house, and none of the files on it had been deleted.

Witness Circles. This classroom circle format is a variation of the fishbowl in which a small inner circle addresses a conflict as a larger *witness circle protocol*

outer circle observes. However, in this case the smaller circle includes an open chair reserved for anyone from the observing circle who has something to say over the course of the discussion. If the chair is occupied, the student sitting there automatically speaks next before returning to the outer circle.

Fifth grade teacher Darla Hamilton invited school counselor Francisco Lopez to facilitate a witness circle to address the ongoing use of harmful and inflammatory language by several of her students. In advance of the circle, Mr. Lopez talked to each of the responsible students individually as well as to a handful of other kids in the class. "I made sure I talked to some other students in the class to get a feel for the extent of what had been occurring," he told us.

When the witness circle was convened, it featured an inner circle of five chairs. Ms. Hamilton sat in the outer circle, and Mr. Lopez sat in the inner circle alongside Natalie, Robert, and DeJuan—a victim, an offender, and a witness. He introduced the class to the circle and reminded them of the norms.

"I asked these three students to begin our discussion today," said Mr. Lopez to the class. "Each of them agreed to be a part of this witness circle to talk about the growing problem you've been having with the use of damaging language in class." He went on to explain that the open chair in the inner circle was available for anyone in the rest of the class who wanted to join the discussion.

For the next 25 minutes, Mr. Lopez led the class through a conversation about the effects of derogatory slurs in class. Throughout the discussion, students from the observing circle would periodically occupy the open chair and contribute their thoughts. The class reached a pivotal moment when Oliver, a student with a younger sibling, sat in the open chair and addressed the group.

"I was just thinking that my dad's always telling me to set a good example for my little brother," he said. "But I'd be ashamed if he heard the way we talk to each other."

A few weeks after the circle had been convened, we heard from Ms. Hamilton. "I wouldn't say the problem has disappeared, but it has certainly decreased," she said. "The witness circle Mr. Lopez led shined a light on a problem we needed to address as a class. I'm starting to hear kids call each other on the language they're using—it's not just me anymore."

building ownership of problems & solutions

The purpose of witness circles is not to come up with a solution to a problem but, rather, to show students that the problem affects more than just the students who are immediately involved. Witness circles can move students to feel more accountable to their classmates and recognize their responsibility as witnesses to harmful behavior.

Victim-Offender Dialogue

Victim-offender dialogue works best for addressing conflicts among small groups of students rather than classwide issues. Facilitators should be neutral and possess the following attributes:

- Empathy
- Emotional intelligence
- Interpersonal skills (especially active listening, negotiating, problem solving, and communicating both verbally and nonverbally)
- Cognitive skills (especially paying attention, auditory processing, and reasoning)

The heat of the moment when emotions are high is not the best time to convene a victim-offender dialogue. As Mullet (2014) reminds us, the parties should be given time to unwind first. It is very important for the facilitator to meet with the individuals involved in advance to assess their motivations and gather facts about the situation. We have found the sets of questions developed by Costello, Wachtel, and Wachtel (2009) to be particularly effective during these initial conversations. The facilitator might ask the offender the following sequence of questions:

- What happened?
- What were you thinking of at the time?
- What have you thought about since?
- Who has been affected by what you have done? In what way have they been affected?
- What do you think you might need to do to make things right?

and might ask the victim the following questions:

- What did you think when you realized what had happened?
- What effect has this incident had on you and others?
- What has been the hardest thing for you?
- What do you think needs to happen to make things right?

you don't force kids into a dialogue

If either the victim or the offender isn't willing to participate in the dialogue, then it can't take place, and other consequences may need to be applied. In our experience, it is rare for students to refuse to participate in dialogue. We recall one offender who refused to participate because she was so embarrassed about what she had done: texting naked pictures of an ex-boyfriend to friends. We had worked with law enforcement, and the student had accepted the consequences (anger-management classes and community service), but she refused to face her friends or her ex-boyfriend in a dialogue.

Eventually, we held a meeting with the student's mother to explain the restorative goal of the dialogue. After a long conversation, she turned to address her daughter.

but try to let them see its value

"You have to own this and move forward," she said. "Running away from your past isn't healthy. If you need to see a counselor first to practice, I'll take you, but I really want you to meet with the other students. I know you're embarrassed, but it sounds to me like this meeting can help you move past that."

The dialogue process starts with the facilitator stating the purpose of the meeting, providing an overview of what happened, and discussing the steps necessary to repair the harm done. The facilitator asks participants to listen closely to one another, acknowledge one another's feelings, and encourage one another to share their thoughts and perspectives.

Skilled facilitators understand that students will sometimes become emotional and defensive during a dialogue. We can recall a dialogue between two 3rd graders during which the offender kept interrupting the victim to deny that he was at fault. The facilitator reminded the students about the norms of the dialogue and reminded the offender that he would have a chance to share his perspective. "Let's listen to [the victim] right now so that we can learn what he experienced," he said. "Remember, it's not about blame. It's about figuring out what to do next."

After students have shared their perspectives, the facilitator asks the students to share any thoughts or feelings that they've had since the precipitating incident and, as Mullet (2014) notes, "recognize their obligations and commit to restore, reconcile, and make restitution, which are real consequences of their actions" (p. 161). In nearly every one of these dialogues, offending students become emotional when they confront the hurt they've caused. Of course, helping these students realize that they can be a better version of themselves in the future is integral to the process.

When the offender has offered a heartfelt apology to the victim and reflected deeply enough to move forward, the dialogue shifts to a discussion

*again
they are
just
kids*

of outcomes. The offender can offer restitution, and the victim can accept this or ask for additional concessions from the offender. Often, students are harder on themselves than the adults would have been, so the facilitator needs to be attentive to the appropriateness of offers to restore relationships and repair harm.

The results of a victim-offender dialogue should be recorded and shared with teachers, counselors, and administrators. Sometimes the facilitator will develop a contract for students to sign before the dialogue ends. We recall the time two middle school boys got into a shoving match and were asked to sign a contract that outlined the steps they were to follow if they got angry again ("I will take 10 deep breaths when I hear something that makes me angry," "We will lunch together for 10 days to get to know each other so that we don't fight again"). The students themselves came up with the steps, and the facilitator simply printed copies for them to sign.

It's important to note that victim-offender dialogues are not usually one-time events. The offender and facilitator will likely need to have several follow-up conversations to ensure that progress is going smoothly; these can simply consist of brief check-ins. The facilitator may also schedule a follow-up dialogue between the victim and the offender to ensure that there are no lingering hard feelings and that everyone has learned a lesson. We estimate that about half of all victim-offender dialogues will require a follow-up meeting of this sort. Sometimes new issues come up during these meetings that can be addressed to forestall much larger issues. For example, in one follow-up conversation to a dialogue about bullying, the victim, 8th grader Rocio, said of the offender, "She doesn't push me in the halls anymore, but she posted on Facebook that I was cheating on my test." This revelation led to a new victim-offender dialogue and an updated contract between the parties.

Sometimes students are hesitant to talk once a follow-up meeting starts. If this happens, the facilitator may prompt them to finish

the following sentence stem: "If you knew me, you would know
_____." Often, students will begin by revealing fairly superficial
information ("If you knew me, you would know that my favorite color
is yellow") before gradually disclosing more personal truths. The
students take turns completing the sentence, adding new information with each turn.

We recall a follow-up conversation between two students whose
initial dialogue had focused on threatening glares that the offender
had been directing at the victim. During the follow-up, after several
turns, the offender said to the victim, "If you knew me, you would
know my dad's in jail and I worry about my mom."

"I'm worried about my mom, too," responded the victim. "My
dad's not in jail, but he left us two months ago, and my mom can't pay
rent." This was the breakthrough that the two students needed and
even led to the two of them becoming good friends.

A colleague of ours once taught us the importance of focusing
on the value of the words *nevertheless* and *regardless* in conversation
with students. For example, if a student says, "I hate that teacher,"
his social worker might respond, "*Nevertheless*, you need to pass
Algebra." Or if a student says, "I'm not going to apologize to her," the
vice principal might respond, "*Regardless*, do you see that you have
caused harm?" Used strategically, these two words have the power
to keep conversations moving.

Figure 5.2 contains a sample form useful for following up on both
victim-offender dialogues and high-stakes conferences.

High-Stakes Conferences

These types of meetings are intended to address serious issues
that may involve family members, law enforcement, or other outside
parties. Young offenders often don't realize that their actions can
have repercussions beyond the parties directly involved because they

5.2 Restorative Conference Follow-Up Form for Staff

Offender and Offense:

Meeting Date and Attendees:

Facilitator: _____

Victim(s): _____

Supporter(s): _____

Commitments and Consequences:

1) _____

2) _____

3) _____

4) _____

Follow-Up Frequency, Duration, and Persons Responsible:

_____

_____

_____

_____

cc:

❏   Student File

❏   Staff: _____

don't recognize the investment that others have made in their social and emotional development.

Elementary school principal Victoria Washington convened a high-stakes conference after discovering that several of her students were caught smoking grass after school. Not marijuana, mind you— actual grass. The school's vice principal facilitated the meeting so that Ms. Washington could participate as a member of the community along with the children's parents. During the conference, the parents took turns expressing their embarrassment at their children's actions. Ms. Washington shared that she was mortified, too. "It made me look like I didn't know what was happening at our school," she said. "How can I guarantee parents that their children are being supervised? I didn't like feeling foolish." The children at the meeting were surprised to hear this. Realizing that they had failed to consider Ms. Washington's point of view, they apologized to her and to their families. By the end of the conference, the group had agreed on a plan for restoration that included having the offenders work on the school's drug awareness campaign. (The students themselves suggested that they not be allowed to go outside for two weeks, but the principal rejected the offer as unnecessary.)

High-stakes conferences don't just happen—they require a lot of work in advance to ensure that the right people are in the room and properly prepared. Sometimes high-stakes conferences are a next step after a victim-offender dialogue has failed to prevent a problem from escalating. As with other meetings, it is useful for the facilitator to spend some time meeting with the parties in advance to familiarize them with the process and the desired outcomes. We want the high-stakes conference to be a positive move forward, not just another venue for arguments.

We once had a student, Drew, who was implicated in the theft of a dozen electronic tablets from our school—a surprising development, as he had built strong relationships with teachers and administrators.

We learned that he had held the door and served as lookout while another student stole the tablets out of an unlocked classroom after school. When confronted by a suspicious teacher, he said he had heard about the crime and offered some false leads. He only admitted his role in the theft after the police were called.

Drew assumed that he would be expelled from school for his behavior, but he wanted to offer a public apology to school staff and repair relationships as best as he could. Dominique suggested to Drew's teacher that they convene a high-stakes conference, and she agreed. Drew suggested that they include Doug in the conference, as he felt that he had seriously damaged their previously trusting relationship, as well as a teacher who agreed to be an advocate for him. An open chair was placed in the center of the circle for anyone who wished to talk directly to Drew.

The conference lasted 90 minutes. Drew offered his apologies, took ownership of his actions, and listened to staff members as they stated their feelings about the incident. Dominique served as the facilitator and regulated the discussion as needed. For instance, when one staff member became visibly angry and began shouting at Drew,

Dominique interceded and restated the norms. Another member of the restorative practices team escorted the angry teacher out of the room and met with her privately so that she could cool down before rejoining the group. Upon returning, she once again sat down in the open chair, apologized for her earlier reaction, and shared the feelings of betrayal that she felt because she had previously advocated on his behalf.

It is important to note what Drew's meeting did *not* accomplish. The goal of this high-stakes conference was not to identify a plan for restitution but to allow the offender to apologize and members of the community to voice their hurt. Looking back, we're not sure how many adults would be willing to subject themselves to what Drew faced. It isn't easy for a 16-year-old to sit before disappointed and hurt adults who cared deeply about him and hear them share their feelings of betrayal. To his credit, Drew didn't offer excuses or attempt to deflect blame onto others.

[handwritten margin note: remember the purpose]

We all left the meeting feeling emotionally exhausted. But the meeting also proved to be a turning point for us as a school community. Over the course of the next several weeks, we worked with law enforcement, Drew's family, and the school board to determine next steps. In time, we decided that he would not face expulsion but would be placed on probation. Drew has had to continue to regain the trust of the staff, but we don't doubt that the high-stakes conference was life-changing for him.

Reentry Plans

The purpose of reentry plans is for students to reenter the learning community with minimal disruption after having to leave class to cool off or be suspended altogether after misbehaving. For example, let's assume that two students in the same class have a fight and are sent to the principal's office. A reentry plan for these students needs to ensure that they both feel welcomed when they return to class. Without a clear plan in place, the students may be labeled as bullies or wimps by their classmates, which is an obstacle to restoration. In this case, the facilitator may convene a formal classroom circle to allow people to express their feelings about classmates fighting in

[handwritten margin note: The goal is to restore relationships]

general. Alternatively, he or she may spend a few minutes outlining any agreements the fighting students have reached and asking for the rest of the class's help in supporting their commitments.

Regardless of the amount of time students have missed, they will find themselves having to reintegrate into the instructional flow of the classroom. The return of a student can be marked with high emotions, and reactions from classmates can trigger further problematic behavior from the student. You have undoubtedly witnessed this: a student returns from the principal's office, and classmates immediately ask, "Did you get in trouble?" Having to relive the event all over again is painful for the student and can undo all of the restorative work that has been invested.

Here are the key steps to take when forming a reentry plan for students.

Rehearse with the student. Discuss with the student how he or she might respond to different scenarios upon returning to the learning environment. (We have found that returning to lunch or recess can be especially difficult, as student conversations aren't as closely monitored.) We like to practice using phrases such as "It's OK now" or "It's over now" with students to answer prying questions from classmates. If students are reentering a classroom after an absence, have them vocally commit to staying there and provide them with actionable feedback and restatements so they can hear their plan again ("So I heard you say that when you're back in Mr. Ford's classroom, you expect there will be some small-group work to do. You stated that you plan to move into the group quietly and follow someone else's lead. That's a good plan.").

Identify a lifeline, if needed. Students returning to class or school from an emotionally charged event may find themselves more anxious or uneasy than expected. In such cases, educators should work with them to identify a "lifeline" they might use in case they need to take a short break upon their return. This might be as simple as a quiet

practice scenarios

request for the teacher to call over a trusted adult if the students feel anxious. (At our school, teachers will send an instant message via their phones or laptops to the staff member that a student requests.) In other cases, the lifeline may be a trusted classmate.

Schedule short follow-up intervals and adhere to them. Checking in with students once or twice a day after they've returned from an imposed absence can help to anchor their days and gives students a safety valve to let off steam.

teachers must be part of the process

Close the loop with the adults involved so that they can more effectively respond to students' emotions. Teachers may have unrealistic expectations for students who have been removed from the instructional flow, assuming that they'll be able to pick right up where they left off. Educators in charge of students' reentry plans should escort their students back to class on their return so that they can apprise teachers both of the students' current state of mind and of the commitments that they've made.

Arrange an end-of-day check-in. These types of follow-ups can provide students with just the excuse they need to peel away from friends who might otherwise escalate their misbehavior. They also give educators one more opportunity to provide students with guidance and positive affirmations.

make this sustainable for the student

Implement the follow-up plan. Long-term change can only be realized when students are able to truly reflect on the harm they've caused and what they have learned since. We are not suggesting that students be forced to dwell on the past forever, but regular follow-up conversations following a major event can reduce reoccurrence and build stronger relationships between students and adults.

Student Voices: "I Became a Better Me"

Impromptu conferences, circles, and high-stakes conferences have a cumulative effect: together, they lead students to discover who they really are, who they want to be, and how they want to live. Investing in their identity development is well worth the effort.

Jordan was a 10th grader who got in a lot of trouble. She said that she didn't know who she was, that she didn't care about herself, and that people only liked her if she made them happy. As a result, Jordan readily adopted the habits and behaviors of others while minimizing her own values and beliefs: she used and sold drugs, stole from others, ditched classes, and cheated on tests (despite the fact that she was easily in the top 10 percent of her class).

Jordan was a long-term project, and many people had invested in her. She was involved in numerous meetings and conferences. Her dad had spent time in prison and didn't want his daughter to follow his path, but he also didn't know how to help her.

"I have my at-home Jordan," he said, "but then when she goes to school she's a different person. She's street Jordan, and she's doing drugs, ditching school, and getting into trouble."

Jordan's father offered to attend any and every meeting at school that had anything to do with his daughter. He also learned how to have productive conversations with her at home that mirrored the conversations she had at school.

Jordan soon came to understand that the adults in her personal and academic life were not going to give up on her, no matter how many times she tried to push them away. She also realized that there were paths back to a healthy road when she got off track. Over several years, she became more self-assured and began voicing her own thoughts rather than worrying about what her friends of the moment would think. As she herself put it, "I was a handful, always trying to please the wrong people. But no one gave up on me. I had to face the consequences, but I wasn't shunned because of what I did. I became a better me, and I'm proud of who I am now. I am going to college and studying marine biology because none of you would let me fail, no matter how hard I tried."

6 | Creating the Mindset for Restorative Practices

We know how important it is for students to understand the relationship between effort and achievement, especially when it comes to overcoming difficult content. We want to disrupt the fixed mindset among students who believe that innate ability and personal characteristics, rather than effort, are the determining factors in academic success. We also want to disrupt the fixed mindset of educators who prefer to pin the blame for their school's failures on the students, parents, or the community rather than to take ownership of them and work to make things better.

Schools with a growth mindset believe in their capacity to change, but it takes more than attending a few professional development seminars and reading some research literature to implement effective restorative practices; the process requires buy-in across the entire school and must relentlessly focus on examining long-held practices.

Creating a Welcoming Mindset

We all know when we're welcome somewhere. Whether it's a family celebration or an appointment at the dentist's office, we expect to be greeted in a certain way—many hugs and kisses at a family celebration, for example (maybe fewer at the dentist's office). When we are expected or welcome, we tend to be greeted by name and with a smile, asked how we're doing, and kindly directed to our destination. Welcoming schools do exactly the same thing.

When ensuring a welcoming mindset, educators should pay special attention to

- The front office,
- Adult points of contact,
- Onboarding of new students and staff, and
- Obstacles to creating a positive environment.

The Front Office

First and foremost, schools need to exude a welcoming atmosphere that is felt by every child and adult in the school. Because the front desk serves as the first point of contact for anyone entering the school, it is especially important in this regard. In many schools, the people working at the front desk are charged with managing a host of processes: screening visitors, answering parents' questions, directing sick children to the nurse's office, and so on. Little wonder that workers often become swamped by such duties and find themselves with little time left for greeting visitors at the counter.

We've renamed the front office manager at our school the concierge because she oversees how visitors, students, families, and teachers are greeted. On days when we expect scheduled visitors, she posts a welcome sign greeting them by name. Our concierge shows student workers how to extend proper greetings and escort visitors to their destinations. When parents or community members show up unannounced, she offers them a comfortable seat before working on a way to accommodate their requests.

Adult Points of Contact

To further create a welcoming environment, we ensure that adults are present in places where students tend to congregate or where there's a lot of foot traffic so that they can greet whomever they see. In fact, we have available administrators staff a small desk in a central location of our school to greet tardy students in the first 15 minutes of the school day. We can tell you these interactions are invaluable. We start by greeting the students, then ask why they are late, and finally let them know that we're glad they are at school. In addition to further reinforcing positive relationships with students, these short conversations help us to distinguish those who are chronically late from the others.

Onboarding New Students and Staff

It took several years for us to realize that students who enroll after the first week of school miss out on a pivotal culture-building period. Nowadays we offer a daylong onboarding experience for such students. On their first day in school, they spend time with a variety of adults and students touring the premises, learning about the school's mission, and asking any questions they may have about logistics. In the afternoon, they sit in on at least two classes and take notes about their observations, which they later discuss in a circle with available staff members as well as student leaders. At the end of the day, the new students receive their class schedules. We feel that this onboarding experience helps students to orient themselves, get a feel for the climate, and begin to establish relationships with adults in the school.

We follow a similar onboarding process with new staff members. Regardless of their job responsibilities, new personnel are required to tour the entire school, sit in on classes, and meet with administrators and student representatives. During this process, they also meet with the school's IT team to register passwords, equipment, keys, and so forth. New teachers are required to spend their second day of onboarding observing their assigned students in various classes to get an idea of how they conduct themselves throughout the day. New staff members can only assume their job responsibilities after at least two days of onboarding experiences.

≡ prioritizing new teachers // culture

Obstacles to Creating a Positive Environment

Sometimes extensive security measures can get in the way of creating a welcoming atmosphere. Although such measures as metal detectors, a campus police presence, student identification badges, and surveillance cameras are meant to inspire a sense of safety in students, one study of their use in schools shows that they can result in more rather than less strife (Bracy, 2011). Many of the students in the study said that they thought administrators implemented school measures simply to flex their power rather than to further student well-being. They also reported that educators focused much more on preventing misbehavior and punishing violators than on recognizing positive behaviors among students.

Administrators at high-security schools need to be intentional about placing staff in areas where they can greet students and visitors warmly. Handshakes, smiles, and pats on the back can go a long way to countering negative perceptions of intrusive security measures. If security guards or police officers are present, they too should help to create a welcoming environment. Many police officers are trained in community policing and understand the benefits of building positive relationships. School resource officers and similar personnel can and should be recruited to act as mentors to students, facilitate police athletic events, and serve as members of school committees (Morgan et al., 2014).

Data Mindset

Information about how a school is doing is all around us; we just need to be intentional about locating, analyzing, and leveraging it for school improvement. The data come in two forms: *quantitative* (the hard data of numbers) and *qualitative* (the soft data of stories). Educators are used to receiving voluminous amounts of hard data, especially in the form of student achievement reports, but rarely do they analyze the reports for deeper meaning and take necessary actions based on their findings. Soft data are essential because they allow us to understand students' perspectives and therefore their actions.

Hard Data

In addition to demographic and achievement reports, schools should regularly examine attendance and disciplinary figures. Other nonacademic data can add dimension to the portrait of a school as well: knowing how often the nurse's office is used, by whom, and for what reasons, for example, can help to reveal underlying chronic health issues. Another overlooked source of hard data is telephone records: Whose parents has the school contacted? Why, and by whom? Schools that track parent contacts by teachers, front office personnel, and administrators are better able to locate gaps in their efforts to build strong community relations.

Disciplinary audits are an excellent starting point for assessing current practices and taking action to improve results. The form in Figure 6.1 includes gender and ethnicity data for students over the previous three years that educators can examine for evidence trends. These data can be used to analyze the effectiveness of past interventions as well as to identify needs. Data should be reported both in terms of raw numbers and in terms of percentages so that any disproportionality can be addressed. Beyond reporting numbers, the questions in Figure 6.1 invite administrators to examine where and when referrals originate so that they can pinpoint teachers who may need more support creating restorative classroom conditions. Surveys should be variously administered to students, staff, and families in order to obtain multiple perspectives. (The National Center on Safe Supportive Learning Environments has assembled a compendium of

6.1 Discipline Audit

Dates of Audit Review: _____ to _____

Grades Analyzed: _____

Occurrences of Suspensions and Expulsions			
	Year:	Year:	Year:
Referrals			
Suspensions			
Expulsions			

Number of Students Suspended by Ethnicity and Gender							
	Black	Hispanic/ Latino	Asian/ Pacific Islander	Native American	White	Multiple	Total
Male							
Female							
Total							

Who are the three teachers who submit the most discipline referrals? _____

_____

Who are the three teachers who submit the fewest discipline referrals? _____

_____

Which grade level or department has the highest rate of discipline referrals? _____

Which grade level or department has the lowest rate of discipline referrals? _____

Are there specific populations of students (e.g., English learners, students with disabilities, students who qualify for free lunch) who receive a disproportionate number of discipline referrals? If yes, describe. _____

_____

Are there specific locations within the school that generate a disproportionate number of discipline referrals? If yes, describe. _____

_____

Are there specific times during the day that generate a disproportionate number of discipline referrals? If yes, describe. _____

_____

Source: Fisher, D., Frey, N., & Pumpian, I. (2012). *How to create a culture of achievement in your school and classroom* (p. 185). Alexandria, VA: ASCD. Used with permission.

surveys for different purposes and intents at http://safesupportive learning.ed.gov/topic-research/school-climate-measurement/school-climate-survey-compendium.)

Most schools have a visitor sign-in book and an early-dismissal log that can be tapped to gather data on how welcoming the school's climate is. Figure 6.2 shows a follow-up survey that educators can use to ask visitors about their experiences on campus.

Possessing a data mindset means having a plan in place to transform information into action. Here are some suggestions for doing so effectively (James-Ward, Fisher, Frey, & Lapp, 2013):

Start early. The beginning of the school year is the traditional time for examining data because it's when many state reports become available. It's also a good idea to examine data after the first nine weeks of school to locate early trends and intervene as necessary.

Look for links between practice and results. As you examine the data, it's helpful to disaggregate them by individuals, grade levels, departments, and so on—not for the purpose of assigning blame but, rather, to locate specific areas of strength and opportunities for improvement. Data teams that fail to go the extra mile to link practices and results risk diffusing their improvement efforts.

Make the findings public and encourage speculation. Reoccurring problems will require coordinated efforts across groups. For this reason, educators should share their data not only with faculty but with students and families as well and should invite suggestions and solutions from everyone to create a shared sense of ownership.

Pay close attention to historically underserved subgroups. Research shows that factors such as gender, ethnicity, disability, family income, and language can predict how often students are disciplined (e.g., The Civil Rights Project, 2000). Examining such data provides educators with a crucial lens through which to consider the application of restorative practices.

Plan regularly scheduled dates to analyze interval data. Businesses track data closely so that they can respond quickly to changing

6.2 School Contact Survey

You recently visited our school, and we would like to find out about the quality of the experience. Your input is very important. Findings of the survey will be summarized and used to improve the school's efforts in strengthening our partnership with all members of our school community.

1. What was the date of your most recent visit? _____

2. What was the nature of the visit? Choose all that apply:

- Picked up my child from school
- Brought my child to school
- Dropped something off for my child
- Visited a classroom (if so, name the teacher: _____)
- Attended a meeting
- District business
- University business
- Community business

3. For each of the following statements, please tell us whether you strongly agree, agree, disagree, or strongly disagree:

- Reception staff were friendly and helpful.
- I was promptly greeted.
- I felt welcomed.
- I was able to fulfill my purpose for visiting in a timely fashion.

4. What else would you like to tell us about your visit to our school? _____

_____

_____

_____

5. How can we improve the experience for you next time you visit? _____

_____

_____

_____

Thank you for taking the time to complete this survey. We can't become the Best School in the Universe without people like you!

markets, yet some schools confine their reviews of data to once per year. Why would we think that working with the most complex of organisms—human beings—is somehow simpler than working with widgets? We actually analyze data throughout the year: we monitor attendance daily, generate weekly grade reports, and issue monthly data on disciplinary actions.

Every year during the back-to-school faculty retreat, we discuss students' academic and behavioral performance. Before we embarked on our restorative practices journey, our school's suspension rates were similar to those of other schools in the neighborhood. And as at those schools, some groups of students were being suspended at disproportionate rates. Although morale among staff was satisfactory, many were happy to see some students kicked out of school. In fact, a former administrator circulated lists of students and asked teachers to rate them so that they could "clean house" of the most poorly behaved students.

It's not that we were a bad school; things were generally OK. Students were punished when they did things wrong, and parents became defensive when informed—probably the same status quo as at the schools around us. But things changed when our philosophy changed. Our suspension rates are now incredibly low, attendance is up, and teacher satisfaction and morale have skyrocketed (even at a time of declining fiscal resources). Teachers now have opportunities to share when they have experienced harm, which leads to healing. It's profoundly moving to watch students attempt to repair any harm they've caused. When we embraced a restorative practices outlook, even parents' attitudes began to change: instead of reacting defensively and trying to get their children out of trouble, our students' parents understand that their children need to learn to behave as citizens and need to realize that the school is there to teach them how.

An Early Warning Mindset

An early warning mindset helps educators to determine whether students are heading for trouble, allowing them to intervene early. In some cases, analyzing data related to individual students can expose problems that they might be enduring in plain sight but that have been overlooked by the school. Over half of U.S. state departments of education mandate early warning reports on individual students to identify possible areas of concern. These reports take into account the following data:

- Attendance rates
- Grade-level promotion or retention
- Course completion rates
- Grade point averages
- State standardized test results
- Student mobility

Schools in states that don't have early warning systems in place can amass this type of information with moderate effort. Additional factors to consider include whether students have disabilities, are English language learners, are in foster care, and are in good academic standing in current classes. Students whose patterns of attendance, course completion, and disciplinary actions suggest that they are at risk for failure should be targeted for additional support.

Figure 6.3 shows a list of early warning signs developed by the California State University system. As a California State University flyer puts it, "Trust your instincts and SAY SOMETHING if a student leaves you feeling worried, alarmed, or threatened!" (n.d.).

As useful as early warning systems can be, educators should use caution when interpreting the signs—after all, data are not destiny. To avoid stigmatizing students, we prefer not to quantify their relative levels of risk (which state-generated reports tend to do). We don't

6.3 Assisting Students in Distress

Academic Indicators
- Sudden decline in quality of work and grades
- Repeated absences
- Disturbing content in writing or presentations (e.g., violence, death)
- You find yourself doing more personal rather than academic counseling
- Continuous classroom disruptions

Safety Risk Indicators
- Unprovoked anger or hostility
- Making implied or direct threats to harm self or others
- Academic assignments dominated by themes of extreme hopelessness, rage, worthlessness, isolation, despair, acting out, suicidal ideations, violent behavior

Psychological Indicators
- Self-disclosure of personal distress that could include family problems, financial difficulties, depression, grief, or thoughts of suicide
- Excessive tearfulness, panic reactions, irritability, or unusual apathy
- Verbal abuse (e.g., taunting, badgering, intimidation)
- Expressions of concern about the student by his or her peers

Physical Indicators
- Marked changes in physical appearance including deterioration in grooming, hygiene, or weight loss/gain
- Excessive fatigue or sleep disturbance
- Intoxication, hangovers, or smelling of alcohol
- Disoriented or "out of it"

Source: California State University. (n.d.) *Assisting students in distress*. Los Angeles: Author. Available: http://www.calstate.edu/redfolder/pomona/Red-Folder-Pomona.pdf

want to inadvertently prime teachers to believe that some students are beyond salvation, and we certainly don't want students to give up, believing that their fate is preordained. Educators should use the early warning system to identify students who need more support and then get to work building positive relationships with those students—fast.

It's not to write kids off; it's to give them extra support

At our school, we pay close attention to new students, especially 6th and 9th graders, in the first week of classes. Administrators are regularly rounding, asking teachers to identify students who might need additional behavioral support. By the first Friday of the school year, we've usually compiled a list of such students—we call them "high flyers"—and each administrator takes on two or three of them as his or her responsibility for the next four years. We devote our energies to building a positive relationship with each of "our" students and serve as their advocates to the rest of the school. Nearly all of the students we've identified early on for support have become important parts of our lives. Of course, we don't disclose to them that we had targeted them for intervention early on, although sometimes we'll let them know as they near graduation (and they *do* graduate). At that point, they're prone to enjoy hearing about their younger, sillier selves. (Many of the stories in this book are from our high flyers.)

A few years ago, Doug was having a conversation in the hallway with a principal visiting from another school when one of his high flyers stopped by and gave him a warm hug. Doug paused the conversation to return the young man's hug, wish him well, and send him on to class.

The principal with whom Doug had been speaking stood there with her mouth agape. "I was that boy's middle school principal," she said. "My co-workers and I used to high-five each other on days when he didn't get off the bus, because it meant we'd have a better day without him there." With that, she broke down in tears.

All of us have probably experienced the secret relief of knowing that a particular student won't be at school today.

Students like Doug's high flyer come to expect that they aren't wanted around, and such a negative self-concept takes a toll. As W. E. B. Du Bois pointedly asked in *The Souls of Black Folk* (1903), "How does it feel to be a problem?" (p. 1). *The way we feel about kids MATTERS*

A Preventative Mindset

Too often, we find ourselves trying to resolve a crisis the moment it arises. Anticipating crises can reduce their impact and accelerate our responsiveness to students, faculty, and families.

Cyberbullying is an area of particular concern that requires a preventative mindset. With increasing regularity, responsive schools are anticipating the problem and addressing it directly in the curriculum. Many police departments, child advocacy agencies, and professional organizations provide valuable materials about cyberbullying that teachers can share with their students. In screening the materials, teachers should consider the following questions:

- Are they developmentally appropriate?
- Are they part of a continuing series?
- Do they teach students through examples and link to the harmful effects of cyberbullying?
- Do they include strategies students can use to protect themselves online?
- Do they suggest what students should do if they are victims of cyberbullying?
- Do they suggest what students should do if they observe cyberbullying behavior?
- Do they address the consequences that cyberbullies should face?

Another way to hone a preventative mindset is to instill awareness about sensitive issues among staff. For example, we require all staff at our school to receive training on issues related to students who identify as lesbian, gay, bisexual, transgender, or questioning (LGBTQ). Because we believe strongly that our school should be a safe space for everyone, there is a sign in every classroom noting that all students are accepted and protected and that damaging language and behavior will not be ignored.

Although some staff members have felt their religious or cultural beliefs challenged by our acknowledgment of LGBTQ issues, we have never encountered a caring educator who opposes the core values of being free of harassment—and being free to learn.

A Team Mindset

Every job in a school comes with a well-defined set of responsibilities: teachers teach, counselors counsel, and administrators administer. Unfortunately, narrowly focused roles are not compatible with a holistic approach to education. The life of a schoolchild touches at various times on every specialization offered at school, but rarely in isolation. To ensure that we take the full complexity of students' school lives into account, we strongly recommend implementing interdisciplinary school teams.

Our school begins each day with a 10-minute standing meeting in one of the larger classrooms during which our informal interdisciplinary teams meet. (We call it a standing meeting for two reasons: because no one sits down, as meetings seem to double in length whenever that happens, and because the meeting occurs every day of the school year.) All the adults on campus, both certificated and classified, stand in a circle and discuss the following three agenda items:

1. Logistics and scheduling
2. Spotlight on students who deserve recognition or are causing concern
3. A culture-building routine

The entire faculty stands in a circle around the perimeter of the room. After a preliminary discussion of logistics and scheduling, the principal turns our attention to spotlighting students. It is at this time that our informal interdisciplinary teams emerge.

Here is an example. One morning, a 10th grade teacher expressed concern about a 12th grade girl whose behavior seemed to be regressing. Within moments, two 12th grade teachers mentioned that they'd already made plans to meet with her for a private lunch, an 11th grade teacher reported on a discussion she'd had with the girl after school the day before, and the girl's athletics coach shared his intention to talk with her on the bus ride home from the next game. None of the adults disclosed any information about the student's difficulties at the meeting, but they were able to identify coworkers to strategize with afterward.

The kinship we feel when we look our professional colleagues in the eye every morning is powerful. Importantly, it strengthens our belief that problematic situations are best addressed through coordinated efforts among staff. Quite frankly, we can't imagine not having a morning meeting each day. Without it, we don't believe we'd be the school we are today.

We know that it's not possible for every school to replicate our morning routine. For some larger schools, it would be impossible to fit all staff into a single room. But what about holding several simultaneous morning meetings? Teachers could be divided up by grade level rather than department for a different perspective. (We should note that our morning meetings are in lieu of faculty meetings, so our staff meet together for a total of 50 minutes a week.)

Although knowing that students are disengaged, feel hopeless about their futures, and do not report daily positive experiences is deeply troubling, the good news is that we as educators possess the power to change these numbers. What if educators made an intentional effort, coordinated across the school or district, to do so? We believe that effective processes for engaging students have the following three key elements:

1. **They are proactive.** Processes should focus on students' communication, collaboration, and problem-solving skills using a strength-based approach, and educators should identify and enact an early warning system to locate students who need more intensive supports.
2. **They are systematic.** Clear guidelines and principles should be in place to govern student interventions.
3. **They are transparent.** Everyone with a stake in the organization, including students, families, and other community members, understands the process and has a voice in refining and customizing it.

Student Voices: "I Have Hope, and a Plan to Get Where I'm Going, Because People Cared About Me"

Gallup, the news and polling agency, is in the business of acquiring and analyzing opinion data that help us to detect patterns and locate trends. In a 2014 release, Gallup Inc. reported survey results finding that student engagement declined with each grade level—a disturbing trend to be sure. But the report offered reasons to celebrate as well. Students who strongly agreed with the statements "My school is committed to building the strengths of each student" and "I have at least one teacher who makes me excited about the future" were nearly 30 times as likely as their peers to be engaged in their school. Gallup also reported that teachers had a direct influence on the degree to which students felt hopeful about their futures. What's more, one-third of students surveyed "who scored highly on all three dimensions that the assessment measures: hope, engagement, and well-being . . . were classified as success-ready" (p. 3).

Brandi was one of those students who exhibited "hope, engagement, and general well-being." Despite growing up in poverty and not scoring very well on her initial assessments for reading or math, she developed a fantastic sense of herself and her future. "I have hope for a better life because people care about it," she told us. "I mean, all those people can't be wrong. I must be a pretty amazing person if they all like me so much. I know that I'm loved, and that gives me hope. I don't want to disappoint the people who love me—or myself. I know that I'm ready to graduate high school and go to college after that. I have hope, and a plan to get where I'm going, because people cared about me."

Conclusion

We will conclude this book the way we began it—with an invitation to learn. Consider how different the fates of the students Gallup surveyed who were not "success-ready" would be if they had regularly encountered intentionally inviting adults throughout the school day. Students who feel hopeful and cared for are able to achieve at higher levels—and the best news is that it is within our power to help them do so.

References

Alberto, P. A., & Troutman, A. C. (2012). *Applied behavior analysis for teachers* (9th ed.). Columbus, OH: Merrill.

Alexander, P. A., & Jetton, T. L. (2000). Learning from text: A multidimensional and developmental perspective. In M. L. Kamil, P. B. Mosenthal, P. D. Pearson, & R. Barr (Eds.), *Handbook of reading research* (Vol. 3, pp. 285–310). Mahwah, NJ: Erlbaum.

Allen, J. A., Gregory, A., Mikami, A., Lun, J., Hamre, B., & Pianta, R. (2013). Observations of effective teacher-student interactions in secondary school classrooms: Predicting student achievement with the Classroom Assessment Scoring System—Secondary. *School Psychology Review, 42*(1), 76–97.

ASCD. (2008). What students want from teachers. *Educational Leadership, 66*(3), 48–51.

Bickmore, K. (2011). Keeping, making, and building peace in school. *Social Education, 75*(1), 40–44.

Bodovski, K., Nahum-Shani, I., & Walsh, R. (2013). School climate and students' early mathematics learning: Another search for contextual effects. *American Journal of Education, 119*(2), 209–234.

Bonfenbrenner, U. (1979). T*he ecology of human development: Experiments by nature and design.* Cambridge, MA: Harvard University Press.

Bracy, N. L. (2011). Student perceptions of high-security school environments. *Youth and Society, 43*(1), 365–395.

Braithwaite, J. (1989). *Crime, shame, and reintegration*. Cambridge, UK: Cambridge University Press.

California State University. (n.d.) *Assisting students in distress*. Los Angeles: Author. Available: http://www.calstate.edu/redfolder/pomona/Red-Folder-Pomona.pdf

Canfield, J. (1986). *Self-esteem in the classroom: A curriculum guide*. Pacific Palisades, CA: Self-Esteem Seminars.

Carpenter, D. H., Flowers, N., & Mertens, S. B. (2004). High expectations for every student. *Middle School Journal, 35*(5), 64–69.

Cassetta, G., & Sawyer, B. (2013). *No more taking away recess and other problematic discipline procedures*. Portsmouth, NH: Heinemann.

Chang, H. N., & Romero, M. (2008). *Present, engaged, and accounted for: The critical importance of addressing chronic absence in the early grades*. New York: National Center for Children in Poverty.

Cipani, E., & Schock, K. M. (2010). *Functional behavioral assessment, diagnosis, and treatment: A complete system for education and mental health settings* (2nd ed.). New York: Springer.

Cisneros, S. (1991). *Woman Hollering Creek and other stories*. New York: Random House.

City, E. A. (2014). Talking to learn. *Educational Leadership, 72*(3), 11–16.

The Civil Rights Project. (2000). *Opportunities suspended: The devastating consequences of zero tolerance and school discipline policies*. Los Angeles: Author.

Costello, B., Wachtel, J., & Wachtel, T. (2009). *Restorative practices handbook for teachers, disciplinarians and administrators*. Bethlehem, PA: International Institute for Restorative Practices.

Costello, B., Wachtel, J., & Wachtel, T. (2010). *Restorative circles in schools: Building community and enhancing learning*. Bethlehem, PA: International Institute for Restorative Practices.

Curtis, C. P. (2004). *Bud, not Buddy*. New York: Laurel Leaf.

Curwin, R. L., & Mendler, A. N. (1997). Beyond obedience: A discipline model for the long term. *Reading Today's Youth, 1*(4), 21–23.

Danielson, C. (2007). *Enhancing professional practice: A framework for teaching* (2nd ed.). Alexandria, VA: ASCD.

Daywalt, D. (2013). *The day the crayons quit*. New York: Penguin.

Deci, E. L., Koestner, R., & Ryan, R. M. (2001). Extrinsic rewards and intrinsic motivation in education: Reconsidered once again. *Review of Educational Research, 71*(1), 1–27.

Deci, E. L., & Ryan, R. M. (1985). *Intrinsic motivation and self-determinaton in human behavior*. New York: Plenum.

Deci, E., & Ryan, R. (Eds.). (2002). *Handbook of self-determination research*. Rochester, NY: University of Rochester Press.

Du Bois, W. E. B. (1903). *The souls of black folk: Essays and sketches.* Chicago: A. C. McClurg.

Dweck, C. S. (2006). *Mindset: The new psychology of success.* New York: Ballantine.

Fisher, D., & Frey, N. (2014). *Better learning through structured teaching: A framework for the gradual release of responsibility* (2nd ed.). Alexandria, VA: ASCD.

Fisher, D., Frey, N., & Pumpian, I. (2012). *How to create a culture of achievement in your school and classroom.* Alexandria, VA: ASCD.

Frey, N., Fisher, D., & Everlove, S. (2009). *Productive group work: How to engage students, build teamwork, and promote understanding.* Alexandria, VA: ASCD.

Gallup Inc. (2014). *State of America's schools: The path to winning again in education.* Available: http://www.gallup.com/opinion/gallup/173615/gallup-releases-new-insights-state-america-schools.aspx

Gilstad-Hayden, K., Carroll-Scott, A., Rosenthal, L., Peters, S., McCaslin, C., & Ickovics, J. (2014). Positive school climate is associated with lower body mass index percentile among urban preadolescents. *Journal of School Health, 84*(8), 502–506.

Grant, K., & Davis, B. H. (2012). Gathering around. *Kappa Delta Pi Record, 48*(3), 129–133.

Hall, P. (2013). A new definition of punishment. *Reclaiming Children and Youth, 21*(4), 22–26.

Hoffman, S. (2014). Zero benefit: Estimating the effect of zero tolerance discipline policies on racial disparities in school discipline. *Educational Policy, 28*(1), 69–95.

Hynes, W. (2014). Meet the family. *Teaching Tolerance, 48,* 48–50.

James-Ward, C., Fisher, D., Frey, N., & Lapp, D. (2013). *Using data to focus instructional improvement.* Alexandria, VA: ASCD.

Johnston, P. (2004). *Choice words: How our language affects children's learning.* York, ME: Stenhouse.

Johnston, P. H., Ivey, G., & Faulkner, A. (2011). Talking In class: Remembering what is important about classroom talk. *The Reading Teacher, 65*(4), 232–237.

Jones, K. (2013). #zerotolerance #KeepingupwiththeTimes: How federal zero tolerance policies failed to promote educational success, deter juvenile legal consequences, and confront new social media concerns in public schools. *Journal of Law and Education, 42*(4), 739–749.

Kilinç, A. (2013). The relationship between individual teacher academic optimism and school climate. *International Online Journal of Educational Sciences, 5*(3), 621–634.

Kohn, A. (2010). How to create nonreaders: Reflections on motivation, learning, and sharing power. *English Journal, 100*(1), 16–22.

Landau, B. M., & Gathercoal, P. (2000). Creating peaceful classrooms: Judicious discipline and class meetings. *Phi Delta Kappan, 81*(6), 450–454.

Leachman, G., & Victor, D. (2003). Student-led class meetings. *Educational Leadership, 60*(6), 64–68.

Lee, H. (1960/2002). *To kill a mockingbird.* New York: Harper Perennial.

Losen, D. J., Martinez, T. E., & Okelola, V. (2014). *Keeping California's kids in school: Fewer students of color missing school for minor misbehavior.* The Center for Civil Rights Remedies. Available: http://civilrightsproject .ucla.edu/resources/projects/center-for-civil-rights-remedies/school-to-prison-folder/summary-reports/keeping-californias-kids-in-school /WithChange.pdf

Lovato, C., Watts, A., Brown, K., Lee, D., Sabiston, C., Nykiforuk, C., & Thompson, M. (2013). School and community predictors of smoking: A longitudinal study of Canadian high schools. *American Journal of Public Health, 103*(2), 362–368.

McKown, C., & Weinstein, R. (2008). Teacher expectations, classroom context, and the achievement gap. *Journal of School Psychology, 46*(3), 235–261.

Meyer, J., Mann, M., & Becker, J. (2011). A five-year follow-up: Teachers' perceptions of the benefits of home visits for early elementary children. *Early Childhood Education Journal, 39*(3), 191–196.

Michaels, S., O'Connor, M. C., Hall, M. W., & Resnick, L. B. (2010). *Accountable talk sourcebook: For classroom conversation that works.* Pittsburgh, PA: University of Pittsburgh Institute for Learning.

Moberly, D. A., Waddle, J. L., & Duff, R. E. (2005). The use of rewards and punishment in early childhood classrooms. *Journal of Early Childhood Teacher Education, 25*, 359–366.

Morgan, E., Salomon, N., Plotkin, M., & Cohen, R. (2014). *The school discipline consensus report: Strategies from the field to keep students engaged in school and out of the juvenile justice system.* New York: Council of State Governments Justice Center.

Morris, R. C. (1998). Conflict: Theory must inform reality. *Kappa Delta Pi Record, 35*(1), 14–17.

Mullet, J. H. (2014). Restorative discipline: From getting even to getting well. *Children and Schools, 36*(3), 157–162.

New Mexico Public Education Department, Quality Assurance Bureau. (2010). *Addressing student behavior: A guide for all educators.* Author: Santa Fe. Available: http://www.ped.state.nm.us

Payton, J. W., Weissberg, R. P., Durlak, J. A., Dymnicki, A. B., Taylor, R. D., Schellinger, K. B., & Pachan, M. (2008). *The positive impact of social and emotional learning for kindergarten to eighth-grade students: Findings from three scientific reviews.* Chicago, IL: Collaborative for Academic, Social, and Emotional Learning.

Perry, B. L., & Morris, E. W. (2014). Suspending progress: Collateral consequences of exclusionary punishment in public schools. *American Sociological Review, 76*(6), 1067–1087.

Potter, S., & Davis, B. H. (2003). A first-year teacher implements class meetings. *Kappa Delta Pi Record, 39*(2), 88–90.

Pranis, K. (2003). *Peacemaking circles: From crime to community.* St. Paul, MN: Living Justice Press.

Purkey, W. W., & Stanley, P. H. (1991). *Invitational teaching, learning, and living.* Washington, DC: National Education Association.

Qualia, R. J., & Corso, M. J. (2014). *Student voice: The instrument of change.* Thousand Oaks, CA: Corwin.

Ratey, J. (2008). *Spark: The revolutionary new science of exercise and the brain.* New York: Little and Brown.

Roderick, M., Kelley-Kemple, T., Johnson, D. W., & Beechum, N. O. (2014). *Preventable failure: Improvements in long-term outcomes when high schools focus on the ninth-grade year.* Chicago: The University of Chicago Consortium on Chicago School Research.

Rosenfield, P., Lambert, N. M., & Black, A. (1985). Desk arrangement effects on pupil class behavior. *Journal of Educational Psychology, 77*(1), 101–108.

Rosenthal, R., & Jacobson, L. (1968). *Pygmalion in the classroom.* New York: Holt, Rinehart & Winston.

Ross, D., Fisher, D., & Frey, N. (November, 2009). The art of argumentation. *Science and Children,* 28–31.

San Francisco Unified School District. (n.d.). *Restorative practices whole-school implementation guide.* San Francisco, CA: Author.

Sapon-Shevin, M. (1998). *Because we can change the world: A practical guide to building cooperative, inclusive classroom communities.* Boston, MA: Allyn & Bacon.

Schmidt, M. F. H., & Sommerville, J. A. (2011). Fairness expectations and altruistic sharing in 15-month-old human infants. *PLoS One, 6*(10). Available: http://depts.washington.edu/eccl/SchmidtandSommerville2011.pdf

Skiba, R. (2000). *Zero tolerance, zero evidence: An analysis of school disciplinary practice.* Bloomington, IN: Education Policy Center Indiana University.

Skiba, R. J., & Rausch, M. K. (2006). Zero tolerance, suspension, and expulsion: Questions of equity and effectiveness. In C. M. Evertson & C. S. Weinstein (Eds.), *Handbook of classroom management: Research, practice, and contemporary issues* (pp. 1063–1089). Mahway, NJ: Lawrence Erlbaum.

Sorhagen, N. S. (2013). Early teacher expectations disproportionately affect poor children's high school performance. *Journal of Educational Psychology, 105*(2), 465–477.

Sprague, J., & Nelson, C. M. (2012). *School-wide Positive Behavior Interventions and Supports and restorative discipline in schools.* Available: http://pages .uoregon.edu/ivdb/documents/RJ%20and%20PBIS%20Monograph%20 for%20OSEP%2010.11.12.pdf

Strang, H., & Braithwaite, J. (Eds.). (2001). *Restorative justice and civil society.* Cambridge, UK: Cambridge University Press.

Toner, I. J. (1986). Punitive and non-punitive discipline and subsequent rule-following in young children. *Child Care Quarterly, 15,* 27–37.

U.S. Department of Education. (2014). *Guiding principles: A resource guide for improving school climate and discipline.* Available: http://files.eric.ed.gov /fulltext/ED544743.pdf

U.S. Department of Education Office for Civil Rights. (2014). *Civil rights data collection: Data snapshot: School discipline.* Available: http://www2 .ed.gov/about/offices/list/ocr/docs/crdc-discipline-snapshot.pdf

Vance, E. (2013). Class meeting variations and adaptations. *YC: Young Children, 68*(5), 42–45.

Wolfgang, C. H. (2001). *Solving discipline and classroom management problems: Methods and models for today's teachers* (5th ed.). Hoboken, NJ: John Wiley & Sons.

Woolfolk Hoy, A., & Weinstein, C. S. (2006). Student and teacher perspectives on classroom management. In C. M. Evertson & C. S. Weinstein (Eds.), *Handbook of classroom management: Research, practice, and contemporary issues* (pp. 181–219). New York: Routledge.

Yeager, D., & Dweck, C. (2012). Mindsets that promote resilience: When students believe that personal characteristics can be developed. *Educational Psychologist, 47*(4), 302–314.

Zehr, H. (2002). *The little book of restorative justice.* Intercourse, PA: Good Books.

Index

Note: Page numbers followed by an italicized *f* indicate information contained in figures.

About the Authors

Dominique Smith is director of student services at Health Sciences High & Middle College, where he also serves as a culture builder and student advocate. He holds a master's degree in social work from the University of Southern California. Dominique can be reached at dsmith@hshmc.org.

Douglas Fisher is a professor of educational leadership at San Diego State University and a teacher leader at Health Sciences High & Middle College. He is a member of the California Reading Hall of Fame and is the recipient of a Celebrate Literacy Award from the International Reading Association, the Farmer Award for Excellence in Writing from  the National Council of Teachers of English, and a Christa McAuliffe Award for Excellence in Teacher Education from the American Association of State Colleges and Universities. He has published numerous articles on improving student achievement, and his books include *The Purposeful Classroom: How to Structure Lessons with Learning Goals in Mind; Enhancing RTI: How to Ensure Success with Effective Classroom*

Instruction and Intervention; Checking for Understanding: Formative Assessment Techniques for Your Classroom; How to Create a Culture of Achievement in Your School and Classroom, and Using Data to Focus Instructional Improvement. He can be reached at dfisher@mail.sdsu.edu.

Nancy Frey is a professor of educational leadership at San Diego State University and a teacher leader at Health Sciences High & Middle College. Nancy is a recipient of the Christa McAuliffe Award for Excellence in Teacher Education from the American Association of State Colleges and Universities and the Early Career Award from the Literacy Research Association. She has published many articles and books on literacy and instruction, including *Productive Group Work: How to Engage Students, Build Teamwork, and Promote Understanding; The Formative Assessment Action Plan: Practical Steps to More Successful Teaching and Learning,* and *Guided Instruction: How to Develop Confident and Successful Learners.* She can be reached at nfrey@mail.sdsu.edu.

Related ASCD Resources: Positive Classroom Management

At the time of publication, the following ASCD resources were available (ASCD stock numbers appear in parentheses). For up-to-date information about ASCD resources, go to www.ascd.org.

Networks

Visit the ASCD Web site (www.ascd.org) and search for "networks" for information about professional educators who have formed groups around topics like "Positive Classroom Management." Look in the "Network Directory" for current facilitators' addresses and phone numbers.

ASCD EDge® Group

Exchange ideas and connect with other educators interested in school culture on the social networking site ASCD EDge at http://ascdedge.ascd.org/

PD Online® Courses

Classroom Management: Building Effective Relationships, 2nd Edition (#PD11OC104M)

Classroom Management: Managing Challenging Behavior, 2nd Edition (#PD14OC015)

Print Products

Affirmative Classroom Management: How do I develop effective rules and consequences in my school? (ASCD Arias) by Richard Curwin (#SF114042)

Beyond Discipline: From Compliance to Community by Alfie Kohn (#106033)

Connecting Character to Conduct: Helping Students Do the Right Things by Rita Stein, Roberta Richin, Richard Banyon, Francine Banyon, and Marc Stein (#100209E4)

Discipline with Dignity, 3rd Edition: New Challenges, New Solutions by Richard L. Curwin, Allen N. Mendler, and Brian D. Mendler (#108036)

The Educator's Guide to Preventing and Solving Discipline Problems by Mark Boynton and Christine Boynton (#105124)

Handling Student Frustrations: How do I help students manage emotions in the classroom? (ASCD Arias) by Renate Caine and Carol McClintic (#SF114068)

Hanging In: Strategies for Teaching the Students Who Challenge Us Most by Jeffrey Benson (#114013)

The Whole Child Initiative helps schools and communities create learning environments that allow students to be healthy, safe, engaged, supported, and challenged. To learn more about other books and resources that relate to the whole child, visit www.wholechildeducation. org.

For more information: send e-mail to member@ascd.org; call 1-800-933-2723 or 703-578-9600, press 2; send a fax to 703-575-5400; or write to Information Services, ASCD, 1703 N. Beauregard St., Alexandria, VA 22311-1714 USA.